# Footloose in the Peak

## Peter Clowes

# In memory of my father
## who loved the Peak

PETER CLOWES was born near Chapel-en-le-Frith and attended New Mills
Grammar School before becoming a junior reporter on a weekly newspaper in
Stockport.  During a long career in journalism he became northern editor of the
Daily Mail and retired in 1987.   Since then he has contributed articles about the
Peak District to many magazines.

Also by Peter Clowes, *The Peak District at War*
published by Churnet Valley Books.

**CHURNET VALLEY BOOKS**
6 Stanley Street, Leek, Staffordshire.  ST13 5HG 01538 399033
thebookshopleek.co.uk
©Peter Clowes and Churnet Valley Books 2004
ISBN 1 904546 07 2

PRINTED BY BATH PRESS

# FOREWORD

Among the greatest pleasures of my life have been visits to the Peak District and particularly that part of it known as the High Peak. I was born in the heart of the hills and have lived most of my life only a few minutes' drive from the heather moors and craggy escarpments of the district that has been described by Crichton Porteous as *"a box-within-a-box region with endless interests"*.

I make no apology for wandering from subject to subject, dipping into history and extolling the delights of the hills and dales. There is a harsh beauty in the drystone walls that spread a network of uneven lines over much of the Peak. The unknown men who built them centuries ago have often been in my thoughts. They give an almost unique solid character to the Peak District.

I have walked along airy ridges and clambered through the dales for more years than I care to remember and this book is the result of my continual fascination with the countryside and its people.

Some of the material in these pages first appeared in articles I wrote from time to time for periodicals. They include: *This England, Best of British, Evergreen, The Great Outdoors, Derbyshire Life* and *The Peak District Magazine*.

P. C.

Drystone walls enclose fields near the hamlet of Bagshaw.

# CONTENTS

THE PEAK

Market day at Chapel in 1915. Not all animals were penned. As can be seen many were tethered on straw spread over the cobbles. The Roebuck Inn, which was popular with visiting farmers, is in the background. It was one of six public houses around the market place at that time.

## Chapter One
# CATTLE DRIVE

My father perched on a hard wooden bench in the village hall and gazed open-mouthed at the image of cowboy film star William S. Hart as he galloped around a herd of longhorn cattle. It was 1915 and "the pictures" had just arrived in the Peak District village of Chapel-en-le-Frith.

The projector, hand-cranked by its owner George Willie Hobson, wobbled precariously on a table at the back of the hall as local doctor James Bennett played a piano to accompany *The Darkening Trail* which flickered above his head on the fly-spotted screen.

My father, who was 12 and worked during his school holidays for his uncle, butcher Walter Simpson, envied Hart and his fellow cowboys as they rounded up their herd in Texan sunshine. On the following morning the young lad was to take part in his own cattle drive, but one far removed from the glamour on screen.

At 6am he was on his way to his uncle's shop in High Street. Across the road, surrounded by no fewer than six public houses, was the ancient village market place, its stone cobbles now covered with stalls and fenced enclosures containing lowing cattle and bleating sheep. Soon the King's Arms wagonette drew in with several passengers it had collected (fare 3d) from the village railway

Butcher Walter Simpson in the doorway of his shop in Chapel-en-le-Frith. The author's father is the small boy next to the sausages.

station. The bell of the 13th Century Thomas a'Becket Church struck eight and smoke from a freshly-lit tap-room fire in the Roebuck billowed over the inn's stone-slab roof.

Police superintendent Andrew Durkan sat stiffly upright in his smart blue uniform in a pony trap driven by village constable John Wilkins. Buyers from as far away as Norfolk would sometimes travel to this Derbyshire market to buy Gritstone and Swaledale lambs. Lengths of rope, spun by Samuel Dakin at his

The Chapel Gate track that leads into the Vale of Edale.  Kinder Scout is on the left, Mam Tor on the right.

primitive plant in the entrance of the Peak Cavern in Castleton, a village just over the hill, were being offered for sale to a group of eager farmers. There was home-made butter in long flat baskets lined with wet muslin, large blocks of salt from the mines of Cheshire, tasty oatcakes brought from a nearby village bakery and, while cattle took their turn to drink at the market place's old stone water trough, grey-haired Miss Maggie Brunt walked amid their hungry owners to sell teacakes from a large wicker basket.

This was the day of the week that my father enjoyed. The village, he often told me, was full of *"bustle and business"* on Thursdays.  He arrived at Uncle Walter's shop in woollen breeches, buckled below the knee, long black stockings and sturdy boots. Walter Simpson was often busy in the back room rubbing salt onto sides of bacon before hanging them on large hooks outside the shop window.

In those days it was customary for young cattle, known as 'stirks', to be grazed and fattened in lush fields for the summer months, while the long grass in their home meadows was mown for winter hay.  Walter Simpson, who kept cattle on a smallholding at Chapel-en-le-Frith, had made arrangements with a farmer in Edale to accommodate his *"four-footed paying guests"* at a cost of £1 for each animal. That was why, after he had purchased a number of cows at the market, he suggested to his nephew that he should drive them over the hills to the Vale of Edale on the far side of the Pennines - a proposal that my father greeted with delight.

Equipped with a stout stick and his favourite dog Jeb, my father collected about 20 Ayrshire and Red Poll stirks from their pen in the market place and, amid much good-natured banter from flat-capped farmers leaning over the market railings, proudly started his cattle drive down the rough crushed-limestone village street.

There was little horsedrawn traffic to impede the drive as father and his charges slowly made their way through Town End and over Sandyway Head. They climbed a narrow lane through the hamlet of Blackbrook and skirted the village of Bagshaw, with its stone-roofed cottages and tiny semi-detached Methodist chapel, until they crossed Stonyford on Gypsy Lane and reached the high country on Breck Edge.

Uncle Walter had instructed my father to drive the cattle along the narrow lane rather than up the main road over Rushup Edge because of the wealth of grazing on the wide grass verges. At the western end of Breck Edge was a triangular-shaped green at which my father paused for half an hour. The stirks crunched the sweet grass while Jeb lay panting in the shade of a wall, occasionally gobbling up pieces of meat that my father pitched to him from his crumpled bag of sandwiches.

The track on Breck Edge along which the cattle were driven.

My father urged his charges on along a narrow green lane that followed the crest of Breck Edge. In summer, flower-speckled meadows stretched away behind drystone walls on either side. Foxgloves, clover, sorrel and stitchwort grew in the shade cast by the walls. Away to the north stood 1,600ft-high South Head and the tumbling heather-clad moors of Cowburn and Kinder. In the valley below lay 13th-century Ford Hall, its granite walls covered in ivy and its limestone coach drive curling through a landscape of multicoloured trees. This tranquil scene has hardly changed today.

Eventually, they crossed the top of the hill and began their descent down a steep track known as Chapel Gate into the Vale of Edale. The whole length of Kinder Scout, a 2,000 ft-high plateau that dominates the northern Peak District, came into view, its rocky fissures and odd-shaped gritstone outcrops brought into sharp relief by a late afternoon sun.

Much of this sheltered cul-de-sac valley was then owned by the Duke of Devonshire who resided 20 miles away at Chatsworth House. The tenant farmers lived in five hamlets or 'booths' - 'a shelter used by herdsman' - stretched in a line along the sunny south-facing side of the valley and they welcomed the income they received by accommodating lay cattle during the summer.

At Manor House Farm, perched on the side of a steep slope, the farmer's wife broke off from cleaning the building's unusual arched windows to provide my father with a jug of cool milk. At Barber Booth he crossed the River Noe and passed a tiny chapel. Here they joined the main valley road that descended from a nick in the surrounding barrier of hills, and he was soon handing over the cattle at Cotefield Farm which Samuel Gee and his family had farmed since the 17th century.

In the Nag's Head Inn at Edale - now recognized as the southern starting-point of the 250-mile Pennine Way - landlord Hives Barber dispensed beer from jugs and took in lodgers at 4s 6d a night for supper, bed and breakfast. It was here that farmers who had driven their cattle over the hills from the west settled down to enjoy well-earned malt refreshment.

My father was unable to partake of such pleasures, but climbed back over Chapel Gate with Jeb at his heels.

*"It was well after dark when I got back,"* he told me. *"I was a bit weary."*

After all, he was only twelve.

The Nag's Head Hotel, Edale, early in the 20th Century. Landlord Hives Barber sits outside the entrance with his pet dog on his lap.

## Chapter Two
# THE VILLAGE CINEMA

The type of cinema shows that my father saw in 1912 had been replaced by sound films when I was a boy in the Peak District 30 years later.  Before the days of television 'going to the pictures' was a regular twice-a-week escape into fantasy.

We shivered in a queue, leaned casually on a poster artist's version of Jane Russell's bosom, shuffled past a fortress-like pay-box into the cinema's stuffy little lobby, and waited in eager anticipation for the second house to begin.  Muffled music and speech reached our ears from loudspeakers beyond the wall.  Then the strains of the National Anthem suddenly blared out loudly as a tight-skirted usherette, swinging her red torch like a military baton, thrust open the curtained doors to send a blast of hot cigarette-laden air sweeping over us.

It cost ls 6d to sit in the balcony - several rows of seats at the rear of the hall, slightly higher than the rest and separated from them by a long fringe of green velvet curtain hanging from a necklace of brass rings - but we schoolchildren invariably persuaded one of the young blonde usherettes to let us slip up the steps with our ninepenny tickets.

Outside, snowdrifts filled the main street of Chapel-en-le-Frith, while frosty pencil-thin beams of searchlights flickered silently across the clouds in search of German planes roaring monotonously overhead on their way to blitz a northern city, but for two magical hours we were transplanted into a colourful world of spectacle, far removed from the dark stone buildings, walled fields and endless winding lanes of the village that was our home.

The Empress Cinema in Chapel-en-le-Frith.  The owner and his family lived in a flat above the foyer.

But the two hours of magic did not always run smoothly at the Empress Cinema.  Hopalong Cassidy's adventures amid the sagebrush sometimes came to a dramatic and abrupt halt.  A sequence of numbers flashed in front of us at the end of a reel, the screen went blank and the only noise was a loud hum as though an angry bee had become trapped in the loudspeaker.

```
┌─────────────────────────────────────────────────────────────────────┐
│  EMPRESS  CINEMA,  Chapel-en-le-Frith                                 │
├──────────────────────┬──────────────────────┬────────────────────────┤
│ Monday and Tuesday,  │ Wed. and Thurs.,     │ Friday and Saturday,   │
│ Aug. 10 and 11th:    │ Aug. 12th and 13th:  │ Aug. 14th and 15th:    │
│                      │ CESAR ROMERO,        │   ROBT. CUMMINGS       │
│  ALICE FAYE,         │ VIRGINIA FIELD       │   SONJA HENIE,         │
│  WARNER BAXTER       │                      │ Everything             │
│                      │ The Cisco Kid        │ Happens                │
│  BARRICADE           │ and the Lady         │          at Night      │
├──────────────────────┴──────────────────────┴────────────────────────┤
│   This Fri. & Sat.: GEORGE FORMBY in "KEEP FIT"                       │
│ NOTE TIMES: 6-30 and 8-45 Every Evening. Matinee Sat. at 2-30  Tel 116│
└─────────────────────────────────────────────────────────────────────┘
```

A typical newspaper advertisement from 1942.

The audience, sitting furiously in the dark, whistled and shouted and stamped their feet on the sloping wooden floor. We climbed on to the backs of our seats and peered through the little glass windows at the rear of the auditorium where the projectionist could sometimes be seen. Eventually, the cinema's owner, Mr Eldred Fletcher, put matters right and the show restarted. I once recall this happening three times during one performance.

Moving pictures first arrived in the Derbyshire hills just before the First World War. There was a considerable stir, for example, in 1913, when the eminent naturalist Cherry Kearton projected scenes of *"his famous hunt in many lands"* at the Hippodrome in Buxton (now a tea-room in the popular Pavilion Gardens). He used a specially installed cinematograph machine.

This small town boasted a newly-erected Picture House by 1917. The long-skirted usherettes wore grey dresses with crisp white aprons and grey shoes. Their hair was kept neatly in place by a band of grey ribbon. It cost 9d for admission, and this included a cup of tea at the interval.

Cinemas were created in village halls. One, grandly named the Picturedrome, attracted audiences to the small stone market-hall at New Mills; another, the Regent in the Constitutional Hall at Chapel-en-le-Frith, mounted its hand-cranked silent projector inside a cupboard-sized wooden box perched on the wall immediately over the entrance door.

Other cinemas in the towns and villages of the Peak included the Cinema and Art Theatre in New Mills, the Princess Palace in Whaley Bridge, the Opera House and Spa in Buxton, the Grand and Majestic in Leek, the Empire in Glossop, the Ritz and Palace in Matlock, the Cinema in Wirksworth and the Picture House in Bakewell. All were showing movies until the 1950s.

One of the Peak District's most enterprising characters in the cinema world was Mr James Derbyshire who worked as a projectionist at the Picturedrome, the small cinema set up in the raised section of New Mills market hall. He hit upon

The Picture House in Spring Gardens, Buxton. It was demolished in 1936 to make way for the more modern Spa Cinema.

The elaborately-lit frontage of Buxton Opera House where films were shown by rear projection in the 1940s and 1950s.

Crowds shuffle into the Cinema picture house at Wirksworth in 1941.

The Ritz Cinema in Matlock was known as the Cinema House when it opened in 1922.

"Old Susan", the solid-tyred Dennis fire engine based in New Mills that tackled the
blazing Tivoli Cinema in Hayfield in 1932. Captain Lampard sits next to the driver.
The flat-capped gentleman on the left is Councillor J.W.Cochrane, former chairman of
New Mills Urban District Council. The firemen at the 'Hague Bar' station are
Esmond Redmill, Frank Hardman, Stephen Rose, James Snodgrass, Wilfred Bagshaw,
Fred Depledge, Edward Tague and Jack Perry.

*Picture by courtesy of Mrs Kathleen Lee.*

the idea of taking snaps of people in the town. These he then projected on to the Picturedrome screen and anyone whose face was "ringed" was awarded a small prize.

But when the First World War broke out, young Mr Derbyshire ceased cranking the handle of the Picturedrome's projector and went off to fight in the trenches of Flanders. When he returned to civvy street he obtained a job as a salesman for a film company. But his ambition was to show films in the outlying villages of the Peak District and, with the backing of a friend, he formed "Derbyshire Movies", travelling around the countryside in an old van and setting up his projector and screen in halls in places as far apart as Longnor and Hathersage, where villagers sat on rows of uncomfortable wooden benches to watch the antics of Charlie Chaplin and the Keystone Cops.

"Derbyshire Movies" must have been a profitable venture because in 1922 Mr Derbyshire built a cinema in New Mills Road in Hayfield which he called The Kozy. A few years later the cinema was sold to a Mr G. Shearsmith, sound equipment and loudspeakers installed and the name changed to the Tivoli. An advertisement in a local guide read: *Motor buses pass the door..... on wet days we are open in the afternoon.*

Early one summer morning in 1932, however, the people of Hayfield who had spent the preceding day celebrating the crowning of pretty Marie Yarwood as the village May Queen, experienced an exciting night. Two young motorcyclists saw smoke pouring from the Tivoli and called out the fire brigade.

At first the New Mills firemen were reluctant to travel along the valley to Hayfield but they eventually started up their solid-tyred motor engine, which was affectionately known as "Old Susan", and drove to the blazing Tivoli with Captain James Lampard standing in the open cab next to the driver still fastening his tunic buttons as he struggled to ring a large shiny bell. The noise rapidly awakened those people in Hayfield not already disturbed by shouting in the street and the shower of red sparks that was now descending on their roofs.

Unfortunately for the firemen they had difficulty locating a hydrant near the Tivoli - the road had recently been re-surfaced and the grid was covered in tar - and when water was eventually relayed to the scene from hydrants at the Toll Bar and in Station Road there was insufficient pressure to control the blaze.

The entire auditorium was destroyed by flames, only the fire-proof wall of the projection room preventing severe damage to the machines. No one knew the cause but it was certainly the end of the Tivoli - the last film to be shown was *The Reckless Hour*!

## Chapter Three
# JANE EYRE'S WALK

It was at one of the Peak District's village cinemas that I first saw the Hollywood epic *Jane Eyre*, which was shot during the Second World War, when opportunities for location filming were limited. I watched actress Joan Fontaine wandering across studio-created moorland that appeared far removed from any countryside I knew in the North of England.

In fact, it is generally known that Jane Eyre's fictitious walk across the heather was based on knowledge acquired by author Charlotte Bronte when she spent a holiday at Hathersage in the Peak District.

In 1845 Charlotte left her home at Haworth Parsonage in Yorkshire to spend three weeks at Hathersage Vicarage with her old school friend Ellen Nussey, whose brother was the vicar. As she sat, pen in hand, looking through her bedroom window at some of the most dramatic scenery in the Peak, her thoughts must have flown to her own journey from Sheffield to Hathersage across those same wild, windswept moors.

Jane Eyre, who is described as living in Yorkshire at Thornfield Hall with the irascible Mr Rochester and his daughter, flees one day at dawn, takes passage on a coach and alights at a lonely crossroads.

The novel is written in the first person. *"Whitcross is no town, nor even a hamlet,"* says Jane. *"It is but a stone pillar set up where four roads meet: white-washed, I suppose, to be more obvious at a distance and in darkness. Four arms spring from its summit: the nearest town to which these point is, according to the inscription, distant ten miles; the farthest, about twenty. From the well-known names of these towns I learn in what county I have lighted; a north midland shire, dusk with moorland, ridged with mountain.*

*There are great moors behind and on each hand off me; there are waves of mountains far beyond that deep valley at my feet. The population here must be thin, and I see no passengers on these roads: they stretch out east, west, north and south - white, broad, lonely; they are all cut in the moor, and the heather grows deep and wild to their very verge."*

Two coach roads, about five miles apart, crossed the Pennine moors near Hathersage in 1845. Many traditionalists choose the Fox House Inn on the road from Sheffield to Hope as the likeliest place where Jane alighted. The author J.B. Firth, who frequently visited the area around 1900, is emphatic on the point. Here the road was crossed by a turnpike built from Grindleford to Penistone in 1775 to permit wagons loaded with wool to reach the Yorkshire mills.

Yet if Jane had alighted at the Fox House and wandered northwards over the moor she could hardly have caught sight of the Hathersage valley and its *"hamlet and spire"* on her right hand. This leads one to suppose that the girl must have left the coach on the more northerly turnpike at Moscar Cross and wandered southwards towards *"Morton"*.

At the cross, a Pennine road between Manchester and Sheffield, crossed a drovers' track running into Derbyshire from the north. At this point stood a whitewashed stone pillar. Sheffield lay ten miles to the east, Manchester about 25 miles to the west.

On a gentle hillock close to today's A57 road stands Moscar Lodge, a handsome stone house built in the late 19th Century as a shooting lodge by the Sheffield steel manufacturer Mark Firth. In the spring, its grassy drive is flanked by banks of brilliant daffodils. A few hundred yards away stands a 7ft high stone pillar, blackened with age. Chiselled into its sides are guide marks to the Bradfield, Sheffield, Hathersage and Hope roads - the latter direction blocked to 21st Century walkers by a high stone wall.

The pillar dates back to 1702 and it was here, in the days before the present A 57 was built, that Jane could well have alighted after a long coach journey from the West Riding by way of the Penistone valley and the back of Strines Edge.

Charlotte Bronte possibly reached Moscar Cross on one of her summer afternoon walks with her friend Ellen. They certainly went up to North Lees Hall, at the head of the valley above Hathersage, on several occasions and from here there are extensive views of the rocky landscape that leads to Moscar Cross.

In his book *The Peak District Companion*, Rex Bellamy cannot decide whether Miss Bronte had Fox House or Moscar in mind, but the Rev. Martin Hulbert, the former vicar of Hathersage, has no doubt about the latter being the site of "Whitcross".

Jane Eyre turns her back on the guidepost and follows *"a hollow I*

Moscar Cross today. This was where Charlotte Bronte's fictitious character Jane Eyre probably alighted from a Yorkshire stagecoach.

The path over the Stanage moors. Was this the route envisaged by Charlotte Bronte for Jane Eyre?

*saw deeply furrowing the brown moorside; I waded knee-deep in its dark growth."*
She hears a plover "whistle". She probably meant the bird's 'pee-wit' call. She may well also have heard the trill of a curlew circling the moor. Both species of bird are frequently encountered here in the summer.

The path below Stanage Edge is well marked today, countless boots having bared the bleached roots of bilberry and gouged a wide channel in the peaty soil. Jackdaws wheel overhead and grey mountain hares with white tails and legs sprint amid the tumbled boulders.

Jane, we read, lies down under the dark gritstone rocks, nibbling her last bread roll and chewing ripe bilberries that gleam *"like jet beads in the heath"* as she dreams of Mr Rochester.

Near the highest step of the edge a flat toad's head of a boulder protrudes over the serrated crags. Another overhang nearby is known as "Kelly's" - at 50 feet one of the highest faces on the ridge - and rock climbers now come each weekend to lace the rocks with as many ropes as the rigging of a windjammer. There is a lordly panorama of peaks away to the west. The view is particularly striking in the late afternoon when the sun is sinking.

Jane Eyre wanders under this desolate edge through the night, at one point sheltering under a moss-blackened crag. In the sunny day that follows she

The vicarage at Hathersage. From a bedroom window author Charlotte Bronte could see
Moorseats higher up the valley beyond the graveyard.

North Lees Hall was occasionally visited by the writer during her stay at Hathersage.
It bears a striking resemblance to "Thornfield Hall" in the famous novel.

The craggy escarpment of Stanage
Edge with a walkers' track along the
top. High Neb is in the background.

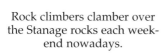

Rock climbers clamber over
the Stanage rocks each weekend nowadays.

eventually hears the chimes of a church bell. *"I turned in the direction of the sound, and there, amongst the romantic hills.... I saw a hamlet and a spire. All the valley at my right hand was full of pasture-fields, and corn-fields, and wood; and a glittering stream ran zig-zag through the varied shades of green."*

She visits *"Morton"* village and, after straying in desperation back towards the moors, she sees a light beaming from a house amidst a clump of fir trees. This is *"Moor House"*, or *"Marsh End"* as Jane sometimes calls it, and the home of Diana and Mary Rivers, who take the wanderer in.

No-one knows which building Charlotte Bronte had in mind when she described *"Moor House"*. It is generally thought to be Moorseats, a manor house about half a mile up the wooded ravine above Hathersage Church and a few hundred yards below Carhead Rocks. The house, still a lonely building of weathered stone nestling behind hedges of yew and holly, has been much altered since the time Jane Eyre was written.

In his book, *In the Steps of the Brontes,* Ernest Raymond comments: *"There is enough in Moorseats to satisfy me that Charlotte was thinking of it when she described Jane's arrival on the kitchen threshold of Moor House.... I found a wall, a wicket and a garden 'dark with yew and holly' just as Charlotte sets forth."*

What is missing from the Bronte description of *"Morton"* is the surprising industry that attracted so many workers from Sheffield, and even Stockport and Manchester, in the mid-19th Century. Hathersage was then an important centre of the needle, pin and wire drawing industry, with no fewer than five mills amid its cottages. According to historian Tom Tomlinson *"there was a constant thick black pall of smoke hanging over the village."*

Nowadays Hathersage is completely different. The mills have gone. Fresh breezes sweep down from the moors. Business people from Sheffield have built handsome houses on the slopes below Stanage Edge, and a steady number of tourists continue to trudge up the narrow lane to the old village church and its neighbouring vicarage. In the village, however, it is unlikely that the arguments about the route Jane Eyre took from *"Whitcross"* will ever die away.

Chapter Four
# LAST OF THE JAGGERS

Stanage Edge, though an exhilarating walk, is not the only escarpment or ridge giving delight to hill walkers in the Peak District's high country. I recall reaching the stony summit of Win Hill on a breezy spring morning and finding six walkers already there, resting their backs on the grey-brown boulders in the wiry heather.

They were a family party from Humberside spending a short holiday in the Peak District. Their bright red anoraks and blue rucksacks looked new and only faint streaks of mud soiled the Vibram soles of their neatly-laced brown boots.

They were having the time of their lives. I had climbed the hill several times but I still shared the joy they were finding in the view from this prominent little summit in the heart of some the Peak's grandest hill scenery.

Although Win Hill is only 1,500 ft high, it forms a handsome pyramid at the eastern end of an airy moorland ridge and from its summit all the major High Peak hills can be seen. The Woodlands, Hope and Derwent valleys are immediately below. If mist does not obscure hills to the north the humpback moors above Holmfirth and the slender TV mast on Holme Moss will be in view.

Win Hill crowns a heather moor which is crossed by a well-trodden track from Hope Woodlands.

The Roman road that climbs the shoulder of Win Hill.

The ancient packhorse bridge crossing the River Goyt that was re-erected higher up the valley when Errwood Reservoir was built in 1968.

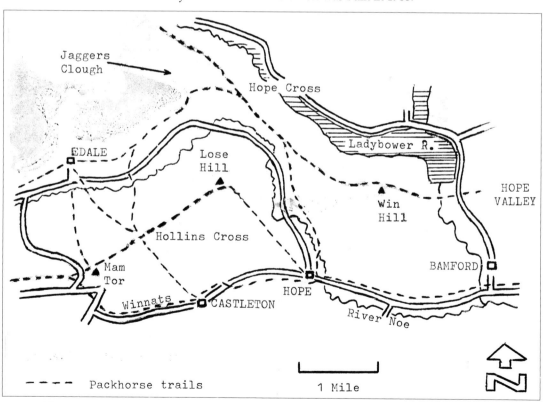

The maze of packhorse trails that criss-cross the High Peak between Edale and Bamford.

A typical train of packhorses
crossing the Pennine moors.

The narrow jaggers' bridge that
crosses the little Grindsbrook
stream in Edale village behind
the Nag's Head.

I joined the family party as they were packing their flasks and preparing to return to their car parked at the side of the River Derwent below. Beyond my outstretched legs was the khaki-green, mirror-like surface of Ladybower Reservoir, with a canopy of dark green conifers on either bank.

My foray to the top of Win Hill was a slight but enjoyable divergence during a tramp that took me along one of the last packhorse trails across the Derbyshire hills. Long before the era of turnpike roads the Peak District was covered by a dense network of packhorse trails over the gritstone moors. Strings of sturdy ponies, weighted down with panniers packed with goods, were a common sight on the crests of the hills surrounding Edale. There might be as few as six carrying salt from Cheshire into Yorkshire, or as many as 50 loaded with lime, coal, groceries, paving stones, even barrels of tar or hogsheads of treacle.

In the days before waggons or coaches were introduced on newly-built roads, it would take more than 300 packhorses to move loads that one juggernaut lorry carries along modern motorways at 30 times the speed today. The horses, in a long line known as a 'jag', would plod slowly along hillside paths that at times were little more than a foot wide. The leading animals wore small brass bells on their collars or bridles to warn travellers ahead of their approach and guide any horses lagging in the rear to prevent them becoming separated in darkness or mist. Each horse wore a 'Devonshire crook' saddle supporting two one hundredweight panniers.

The railway did not reach Edale and the Hope Valley until the end of the 19th Century. In 1850 teams of 50 or more horses were common in Sheffield. Although the transport of salt and coal had almost vanished, milk churns were still being carried by strings of packhorses out of the Derbyshire dales in 1870.

I left the public car park at Edale and headed south-east across the meadows towards the long,dark ridge that links Mam Tor with Lose Hill. It was along this panoramic ridge that the last packhorses probably made their way more than 100 years ago. The main route from the Hayfield-Tideswell trail, near Chapel-en-le-Frith to Yorkshire, left the ridge near Mam Tor and dropped down the Winnats gorge to Castleton and Hathersage. But many 'jags' kept to the crest and reached Hope via Lose Hill.

The only blemish on the wonderful scenic views from the summit of Lose Hill - where there is a useful circular topograph - is a ghastly cement works at the side of the valley beyond Castleton. In recent years a mammoth chimney, from which clouds of grey smoke billow, has been built and there seems no end to the quarrying operations at the edge of Bradwell Moor despite a careful watch by the Peak Park Board. But then the works has been there for more than 70 years and it provides employment for many local people.

From the foot of Lose Hill there is a narrow tree-shaded lane - an old Roman

Ladybower Reservoir - seen from Derwent Edge with tree-cloaked Win Hill beyond.

Back Tor is a prominent feature on the packhorse trail along the Great Ridge.

The packhorse trail along the Great Ridge that runs from Lose Hill to Mam Tor

road - that climbs up the shoulder of Hope Brink to Hope Cross on the slender saddle linking the mass of Kinder with Win Hill. Hope Cross was an important guidepost for the packhorse drivers. It was at a crossroads and even today the squared capstone on top of its eight foot high gritstone pillar reads: *"Sheffield, Hope, Edale, Glossop, 1737."* The last packhorses, loaded with timber, corn and linen, plodded past here on their way to and from Glossop.

The horses were in the charge of 'jaggers' who wore wide sou'wester-type hats to protect them from the inclement Pennine weather, and carried long sticks. They got their name from the sturdy German jaeger ponies they owned. Their progress was slow; it might take them a week to travel from Sheffield to Manchester or Liverpool.

Each evening they would head for a village inn, unload their panniers and tether the horses. We can still find Packhorse Inns on the main routes at Hayfield, Chapel-en-le-Frith, New Mills, Little Longstone and Crowdecote (where a packhorse saddle has been preserved) and a Scotsman's Pack Inn at Hathersage. Also in Hathersage is Gatehouse, a private house that was formerly a farm on an

The zig-zag climb that the jaggers faced at Jacob's Ladder at the head of the Edale valley.

old road from Curbar to Bamford - in the 18th Century it was the Packhorse Inn and mine host Francis Rogers kept a large stable of packhorses for use between Sheffield and Manchester.

From Hope Cross it was a steady walk up the slope to the summit of Win Hill and from there I dropped down into the dale and tramped along the road back to Edale. I could see the chunky spire of Edale Church emerging from a low raft of blue mist over the valley. Beyond was the loaf-shaped mound of Mam Tor, its gullies splashed here and there with small patches of snow. I now walked past Edale's quaint stone bridge, over which packhorses would head along the valley towards Hope Cross, and happily gained the bar of the Old Nags Head.

It is comforting to know that the packhorse trails, criss-crossing the Peak, are giving so much delight to countless country walkers today, many years after the last jagger plodded over these blustery heights.

Stone-roofed cottages cluster around the parish church in Edale. The Kinder plateau looms behind.

Three Shire Heads .

## Chapter Five
# THE FIGHTERS' ROAD

It was not only trains of pack-ponies that trailed over the wilder parts of the Peak in days of old. When the shadows lengthen over Panniers Pool, a favourite resting place for jaggers on their way across the hills between Buxton and Leek, and the infant River Dane gurgles and splashes under a simple stone bridge, it is difficult to visualise the rowdy scenes that occurred at this spot 130 years ago.

Three Shire Heads, where the counties of Derbyshire, Cheshire and Staffordshire meet, lies deep in a remote gorge of the Peak District and it was here, on a small, sandy arena at the side of the Dane, that the "Burslem Bruiser" met the "Preston Pat" in a memorable prizefight in the 1870s.

This tranquil dell, where the Dane valley is hemmed in by high moorland on three sides, became a popular venue for the betting fraternity in the 19th century. By the 1860s, when the public were becoming disgusted with the brutality and unfair practices of professional 'bruisers', the laws against bare-knuckle prizefighting began to be more rigidly enforced.

Marquis of Queensbury rules were introduced and prizefighting became illegal. Nevertheless, its popularity in country areas took some time to evaporate, particularly when purses as high as £200 were on offer.

Three Shire Heads was chosen for the Burslem v. Preston contest because both contestants and the shouting crowd around the roped-off ring, could skip across the county boundary in a few strides, if local constables turned up.

On this occasion, a Leek magistrate heard about the fight and arrived as the pugilists were toughening their gnarled fists in a bucket of pickling solution. When he sternly banned the fight within the county of Staffordshire, the crowd merely stepped across the stone-arch bridge into Cheshire. If a Cheshire county JP or constable had arrived they would have crossed the stream again into Derbyshire.

It is recorded, incidentally, that the Leek magistrate followed the crowd and apparently became an enthusiastic punter with them. Who won the contest history does not say.

Many prizefight enthusiasts who flocked to Three Shire Heads came from the Macclesfield and Buxton areas, and they approached the dell on well marked tracks, crossing wild, squelchy moorland that forms the watershed of the rivers Goyt, Dove, Manifold and Dane.

Starting from the Cat and Fiddle Inn - a famous landmark in this part of the Peak, and at 1,690 feet above sea level the second highest inn in England - I have walked along "the fighters' road" on several occasions.

Typical prize fighters in action before a crowd of punters in the 19th Century.

The lonely Cat and Fiddle Inn on the old turnpike between Buxton and Macclesfield and the sign on its wall.

Curlew circling low over Whetstone Ridge trill loudly as the wind moans over an ocean of trembling heather and stubby grass. Fold after fold of bare hills stretch away on either hand and the flat, hazy plain of Cheshire can be seen beyond the Matterhorn-shaped mound of Shutlingsloe. The traveller Edward Bradbury, who visited this *"savage wilderness"* in 1883, claimed it was possible to see seven counties on a clear day.

A track leads down a steep slope into the valley of the Dane. Piles of shattered stone, torn from the face of Reeve Edge, one or two dilapidated huts and a couple of stubby chimneys rearing out of the heather-covered hillside, are all that remains of busy quarries that were once active in this remote spot.

A narrow terraced route runs along the 1,300 ft contour and swings around the western extremity of Axe Edge Moor. Soon the wide, rocky packhorse trail drops down the side of a stream to Three Shire Heads.

From here the valley widens, providing extensive views over Knar Farm to High Forest and the jagged skyline ridge of the Roaches in the blue distance.

Knar is strictly a working farm nowadays, but an old man sitting in the sunshine outside the door of Turn Edge Farm once told me how he had camped in a field below the stone buildings 50 years before.

*"Mr Slack charged a shilling for bed and breakfast - with two eggs and lots of bacon,"* he said. *"I remember the farm kept a yellow cockatoo which they put outside on its perch in nice weather."*

The summit cone of Shutlingsloe, probably the most distinctive peak in Cheshire, peeps over the saddle between Cut-thorn Hill and its western neighbour, Tagsclough Hill.

The infant River Dane topples over boulders at Three Shire Heads.
Prize fights were once staged in the clearing on the right.

Far down the valley the winding River Dane vanishes amidst thick woodland carpeting the misty eastern slope below Roach End. Just in view is the roof of Gradbach Mill, now restored as a youth hostel but at one time spinning flax and powered by an enormous waterwheel. Two hundred people were employed here then.

The path, along which the Burslem Bruiser's supporters would travel on their way from the Potteries, is now of firm sand and flinty rock. It turns north past the isolated little dwelling of Hawk's Nest but a zig-zag and rather muddy track across the foot of the valley climbs past a waterfall to gain a lane running from Quarnford to Flash, the houses of which lie only half a mile ahead over the hill.

Flash can fairly safely claim to be the highest village in England. It became notorious in the 18th century for its pedlars or 'flashmen', and its reputation for making counterfeit coins of pewter, known as 'flash' (or forged) money.

I have bought excellent roast beef sandwiches inside the tiny black-beamed bar of the New Inn. The writer William Adam had breakfast here in 1850 and *"had no reason to complain of the fare and the obliging attention of the hostess"*.

Knar Farm with the Roaches beyond. Here a cockatoo often amused passing walkers in the 1930s.

A few yards past the high distinguished-looking Wesleyan chapel, which is now a private house, a field path turns north and leads over Oliver Hill - at 1684ft the highest hill in Staffordshire - along the route of yet another ancient packhorse way.

At Dane Head, a shallow, spongy saddle where a shooters' motor track crosses the path, the trigpoint can be seen on Axe Edge, only half a mile over the hummocky, yellow grass and purple heather. *"All around is the spell of silence, the sense of space, the scent of thyme and heather,"* wrote Edward Bradbury.

But even he was afflicted by sportsmen who to this day crouch in small butts to butcher the cackling grouse. *"Once or twice the reverberating ping of the breechloader is heard, and sportsman and smoking tube of steel are seen in relief against the sky"*.

Luckily it was spring when I first crossed Axe Edge, and too early in the year for the shotgun fraternity. Neither did I see Bradbury's *"rustic bilberry gatherers"*, although several motorists were picnicking at the side of the Cat and Fiddle road as the lonely pub came into sight once again.

Axe Edge, a rather dull hill rising to 1807ft, spawns the Dove, Manifold and Wye. On a clear day, the Welsh mountains can clearly be seen, and when the original Ordnance Survey was undertaken, in 1842, a powerful reflector placed on the top of Lincoln Cathedral 70 miles to the east was observed by the surveyors.

The old turnpike that meanders from Burbage to the Cat and Fiddle is a fine walking track. Weatherbeaten stone walls, frequently in ruins, line the path which is about thirty feet wide and metalled with small stones, although much of it is overgrown with tall, lank grass.

Walks along "the fighters' road" are invariably rewarding and invigorating, particularly on a spring day when Goyt's Clough is finally crossed and, as the sun settles low over the distant plain, the traveller again reaches the comfort of the Cat and Fiddle.

The New Inn and parish church in the tiny village of Flash.

## Chapter Six
# DALE O' GOYT

It was from the Cat and Fiddle that I turned my back on the buzzing traffic on the A537 road and followed an old turnpike behind the former coaching inn. The sun shone from a sky streaked with thin, silvery wisps of cottonwool cloud on one of those Peak District days one never forgets.

The turnpike, between Macclesfield and Buxton, was constructed in 1759 and its grass-covered mounds on either side could be seen quite clearly. It was a splendid start to a healthy tramp around the Dale o'Goyt.

I strode on across a corkscrew lane that accompanies the Goyt stream (cars are barred from entering the valley at this end) and followed the old turnpike over the Moss towards Burbage Edge. This is a fine walking track. Weatherbeaten stone walls, with many gaps through which Dale o'Goyt sheep, together with Swaledales and Suffolks, stepped on nimble feet, lined my path.

Shortly after passing an ancient milestone leaning at an angle of 45 degrees, I took a path to the left, leaving the turnpike at a crest, and found a meandering trail - surprisingly not marked on OS maps - through the heather towards Burbage Edge, which is easily recognised by a wall and a copse of stunted thorn trees along the summit ridge.

The corkscrew lane, bordered by old stone walls, that crosses
the moor between the Goyt Valley and Cats Tor.

The track of the old Cromford and High Peak Railway, now a walkers' path, alongside Taxal Reservoir.

The view of wild moorland from the summit cairn on Burbage Edge.

The Goyt Valley in 1967, shortly before the area was flooded to create Errwood Reservoir.
Goyt's Bridge is still in place on the left; the ruins of Errwood Hall lie above the new viaduct.

From the trig pillar I continued walking northwards, the path now hugging the wall, and looked ahead at the southern lip of Combs Moss about three miles away. The west-facing escarpment immediately above White Hall Outdoor Centre jutted up to fill the skyline as I dropped rapidly towards the old railway track emerging from Burbage Tunnel.

The Goyt reservoirs glittered in the sun and the tinkling sound of Wildmoorstone Brook, flowing down a gentle gully into Errwood lake, greeted me as I came off the open moor almost alongside the old stone arch of the tunnel mouth.

The Cromford and High Peak was one of the craziest switchback railways ever built in Britain. It crossed the high moors to link two canal systems. Teams of horses, replaced by locomotives some years later, hauled trains around twisting curves on level sections of the route but gave way to stationary steam engines when steep inclines at Whaley Bridge, Shallcross, Bunsal, Hurdlow, Middleton and Hopton had to be negotiated. Passengers usually alighted and walked up the slopes. Little wonder that the journey of 33 miles from Whaley Bridge to Whatstandwell took at least five bone-jerking hours.

The half-mile tunnel, built in 1830, is still in good condition but locked doors bar walkers who wish to follow the route of the historic railway further.

It was not too difficult to visualise the scene when clattering trains burst out of the tunnel and headed for Bunsal Top. Bradbury described a journey on the *"jerking, jolting"* Cromford and High Peak in his book *All About Derbyshire*. *"We seem to be moving along the top of the world..... it is a scamper across savage and solitary moors."*

A level, terraced track formed an embankment above the valley. From 1831 until about 1894, when the track was abandoned, a stone engine house stood near this spot and a good supply of water was required for its steam engine that hauled loaded goods wagons up a long steep gradient from the valley floor. This was the Bunsal Incline, the steepest on the line with a gradient of 1 in 7.

When the Goyt Valley's upper reservoir was built in the 1960s, a tarmac road was laid down the incline.

Within a few minutes I had reached the foot of the slope and taken a wide, sandy path leading through beech and silver birch, with the towering mound of Errwood dam behind my left shoulder. The sun cast strong shadows ahead of me as I followed the old railway route alongside Taxal Reservoir. Soon I reached the smoothly-pointed walls of a farm access lane that crossed the Taxal dam and, leaving the rail route to meander out of sight amid the conifers of a large plantation, I strode down a steep, grassy slope to reach the River Goyt, crossing meadows and walking through patches of light woodland. All the time the serpentine Goyt sparkled and winked through the trees on my left.

There were masses of pink willow-herb and tall thistles on the banks of the stream; also great stalks of white cow-parsley, some of it almost high enough to hide contented cows that sat in the shade of large, leafy beeches.

At Taxal, where the Goyt swung around a small weir and flowed onwards through a field of dandelions and more tail-flapping cattle, I crossed a narrow wooden bridge and walked up a stony lane to the hamlet and its ancient square-towered church.

The lane was a saltway in the 18th Century, a route along which pack ponies carried panniers of rock salt from the Northwich mines in Cheshire and across a ford at Taxal to Chapel-en-le-Frith. The drovers paid a toll of ¹/₂d each pony before being allowed to proceed over the Pennine hills to the expanding mill towns of Yorkshire.

My route led me south along the shoulder of the hill above Park Wood and I was soon climbing past the stone barns of Overton Hall Farm, which is perched on the edge of Mill Clough. Rhode Island Reds scratched under the rusty shares of a mechanical plough and cats prowling out of the shippons blinked in the sun. It was here that Overton Hall stood in the days of King John.

The Downes family, who were lords of the manor in the 13th Century, held court in the hall. They liked to boast that they had the right to hang and draw criminals, which they frequently did. But the old hall was demolished early in the last century and the present farm buildings built in its place.

I climbed up the hill and hopped over a stiled wall on to an open gritstone ridge where climbers were clambering on Windgather Rocks.

A refreshing breeze gushed into my face from the Cheshire Plain which lay beyond the next ridge. On a lane below, several cars and mini-coaches were parked and more climbers, festooned with coils of rope, their harnesses dangling with ironmongery, were walking towards the foot of the rock face.

This edge is only of moderate height, but is recognised as one of the most useful training grounds for aspiring rock climbers in the Peak. Before the area was opened to the public, a local farmer who owned grazing rights went to great lengths to discourage *"climbing pests"*. He poured tar over the more popular sections of the crags and even chipped off some of the holds. The eminent climber, Joe Brown, recalled: *"If he caught you on the rock face he would throw stones and deliver a torrent of abuse until you fell off or scrambled to the top and ran away."*

From Windgather I kept to the ridge, walking due south for three miles. At first, a wire fence marking the western edge of Goyt Forest lay on my left. A stone wall on the right limited the view across Todd Brook valley with its small, scattered farms until I reached The Street, an old Roman road.

Ridge walks are invariably rewarding and this was no exception. The ground was a mixture of spongy, black peat, tufty heather and short, tough moorland grass.

The stone shrine sheltered by pine trees on the moors above the ruins of Errwood Hall.

The dark rocks that rim the summit of Shining Tor.
The Macclesfield to Buxton road winds below, the peak of Shutlingsloe is beyond.

Several Derbyshire Gritstones were grazing placidly as I walked by. They were well-entitled to be there. These hardy sheep, now widespread in the Pennines, were first bred here - and were formerly known as Dale o'Goyt sheep.

The shallow saddle between Cats Tor and Shining Tor, at 1800ft the highest point on the ridge, proved to be marshy, recent heavy rain having left the moorland squelchy underfoot, and I elected to pick my way along a series of stepping stones removed by former walkers from a dilapidated wall that borders the path.

It was a gentle climb to the summit of Shining Tor, which is on private land just beyond the wall. A stile gave access, however, and I sat on the jagged escarpment rocks to look down on heavy lorries grinding up the A537 road from Macclesfield. The road swept across the foot of the hill like a long, grey snake. Over a grassy ridge to the west the Cheshire Plain stretched towards a hazy skyline where it met the Irish Sea.

A small, dark dish stood out from a patchwork of fields like a tiny bobbin of cotton on a velvet tablecloth - the great radio telescope at Jodrell Bank near Holmes Chapel, about 12 miles away - and the prominent peak of Shutlingsloe above Wildboarclough thrust itself into a clear blue sky to the south.

I turned south-east and followed another wall across open moorland - again having to negotiate a deeply-rutted area of marsh and black, sticky peat on convenient flat stones - to gain a well-trodden track that climbs up Stake Side on the western edge of Goyt's Moss.

This spur provides an easy route down to Errwood Reservoir. Between it and the Shining Tor ridge lies Shooters' Clough, a tree-filled ravine in which grey squirrels and long-tailed tits are seen.

In the trees that cluster around the foot of the ravine are the remains of Errwood Hall. In the last century there were many small farms and cottages in the Goyt Valley. The Grimshaws, a prominent Roman Catholic family, lived in considerable luxury in the hall, entertaining large parties of guests in the grouse-shooting season, and possessing their own coal mine and an ocean-going yacht.

They had many foreign servants. Some of their graves, including that of the captain of the yacht, I found in a tiny overgrown cemetery surrounded by masses of rhododendrons and azaleas on a knoll just above the ruins of the hall. One servant, a Spanish girl named Dolores, employed by Mrs Grimshaw as a personal companion, was so loved and respected that when she died in her forties in 1889 a small stone shrine was erected in her memory at the head of a remote moorland dell a mile north of the hall.

I turned my back reluctantly on Shooters' Clough and walked south across the moor. What a wonderful day it had been. The tramp was typical of the many excellent hill walks that the Peak District offers.

The valley of the Derwent, now sunk under Ladybower Reservoir, seen from Whinstone Lee Tor.

The moors of Kinder stretch away from the Wheelstones on Derwent Edge.

## Chapter Seven
# VALLEY OF LAKES

If a combination of still water and lofty ridges is one's idea of perfect walking country, the High Peak of Derbyshire calls out to be explored, and perhaps the most dramatic lakeland valley is the Upper Derwent Dale, the meadows of which were flooded in the early 20th Century to supply Derby and Nottingham with water.

But when I came across a thin yellow-paged book in a Manchester junk shop, one of several 'penny guides' to the countryside published by Abel Heywood and Son 100 years ago, I became eager to learn what the Upper Derwent Valley looked like before the giant reservoirs were built. The guide, incidentally, cost an extra penny when it included a *"beautifully engraved"* map.

There were advertisements for bottles of Dr J. Collis Brown's Chlorodyne *"for your travelling trunk"* (it apparently acted *"like a charm in diarrhoea and other complaints of the bowels"*) and Fry's Pure Breakfast Cocoa (4$\frac{1}{2}$d per $\frac{1}{4}$lb tin), *"one of the choicest items on nature's menu."*

Several walks in the Peak District were described. One in particular caught my eye - from the village of Ashopton, along Derwent Edge and back down the valley. I decided to follow the route to see what it was like today.

The penny guide to Kinder Scout (with map, 2d) which describes a walk through the Derwent valley villages that have now been submerged.

Until 1945, Ashopton was a village on all the Derbyshire maps. Now it lies buried beneath Ladybower Reservoir, that sprawling spider-shaped stretch of water lying in the Ashop and Derwent valleys above Bamford.

The nearest I could get to this once-sylvan little hamlet, with its stone inn, Methodist chapel and toll-bar cottage, was to lean over the parapet of a great concrete viaduct that was built high over the Ashopton rooftops in 1943 to carry the main A57 road from Glossop to Sheffield.

The inn was a handsome Georgian building with ivy growing up its walls, neat small-paned windows and a row of shrubs in tubs lining the dusty road. Once upon a time stagecoaches had paused outside its pillared doorway before starting their long climb over the Snake Pass.

"At the Ashopton Inn you will find a good cook, decent meals, a bathroom with hot water and plenty of stabling," wrote a Derbyshire traveller in 1905. Weekend ramblers enjoyed Hovis teas provided by the licensee, Mrs Bradwell. But in 1943 Mrs Bradwell had departed, together with her neighbours Percy Law, the village butcher, Joe Marshall, the joiner and Mrs Edith Ayres, who ran a petrol station with hand-cranked pumps nearby. By the end of the year, the waters behind the new dam wall were lapping around the ruins of their former homes.

The Abel Heywood guide gave worthy advice to the walker starting out from Ashopton: "Have a substantial breakfast. Every member of the party should be provided with a stout walking stick and a well filled sandwich-box. Umbrellas, unless used as walking staffs, are needless and useless... if a storm should come on they will be whirled away into the realms of space."

I could well understand the anonymous writer's fears - a strong west wind hurtling over the viaduct threatened to tear the guide from my hands.

The guide recommended the walker to take the Sheffield road past Ladybower Bridge. But this stretch of the A57 - it was one of Thomas Telford's last turnpikes - has been completely rebuilt as far as the Ladybower Inn, and I chose to turn off through a wooden gate and follow a walled track around the corner and through a copse of birch and alder.

After briefly touching the A57 to skirt the front of the inn I walked up Telford's old road, still clearly fenced but its rough stones now overgrown with hummocks of wiry grass, and I climbed up through more trees to gain the open moor below the south end of Derwent Edge. At length I arrived on a low knoll overlooking Cutthroat Bridge, where the main Sheffield road from Moscar crosses the Ladybower stream before dropping in corkscrew style through a gorge to the dam below.

The bridge - a new one was built some years ago, but the stone abutments of the original structure are still in view a few yards upstream - apparently got its name in the 17th Century when someone reported finding "a man with a wound in his throat.... we carried him to the house at Lady Bower."

I consulted the guide: "With permission turn off to your left and, working

The Salt Cellar, weathered by wind and rain over the centuries, on Derwent Edge.

*rather backwards head towards the highest ridge."* This was steady going along a well-trodden path over dark peat and bleached roots of thick heather covering the moor. Two curlews, calling eerily, flew around me in wide circles only feet above the ground. A buzzard drifted high in the sky above a dark scar of rocks rimming the top of the slope.

That westerly wind I had encountered down in the valley now hit me in the face as l breasted the shoulder of the moor. I turned north towards the weathered grey rocks of Whinstone Lee Tor and looked down on the blue-green water of Ladybower Reservoir. It filled the valley between Derwent Edge, on which I now stood, and the sheep-studded pastures of Crook Hill.

From Back Tor, a jumble of rock slabs at 1,765ft, one can follow the watershed over bleak moorland to Featherbed Moss and Margery Hill - a route to be avoided in doubtful weather - but I headed north-west towards the valley at the foot of Abbey Clough. Ahead lay the steep brown slope of Howden Moor, a wild, exposed stretch of yellow grass and dark patches of heather that was the centre of a dramatic search drama in the 1950s.

An elderly shepherd, Mr Joseph Tagg, left his home at Yorkshire Bridge, near Bamford, and walked up the valley to search for sheep missing in the December blizzards that had swept these bleak hills. With him was his 11-year-old Border collie bitch Tip. No one saw Mr Tagg again, although search parties, assisted by ramblers and RAF Mountain Rescue men, spent days on the Howden Moors.

Then, three months later, in March 1954, a farmer rounding up sheep on Ronksley Moor found the dog, looking weak, wet and thin, lying at the side of its master's body. She lived for two more years. Now she has been buried on the

The "Dalek" rock on the craggy escarpment of Derwent Edge.

Ladybower Reservoir with Bamford Edge beyond.
Below the viaduct lies the submerged village of Ashopton.

moors and a stone monument *"for fidelity"* erected in memory of Tip on the roadside near Derwent Dam.

*"Gamekeepers traverse this region to a conspicuous extent,"* warned the Heywood guide. Now, of course, there is no such threat.

When I reached the stone parapet of Howden Dam, where creamy curtains of water were falling down its precipitous face of dressed stone, I consulted the guide. *"Return to Ashopton along the riverside,"* it told me. At the turn of the century, of course, none of the reservoirs had been constructed. A lane - part of the old drovers' route from Hope to Penistone - used to run through the valley alongside the sparkling River Derwent..

The memorial to sheepdog Tip that stands at the side of Derwent Reservoir today.

I ruminated on the changes the Derwent valley had seen since the Heywood guide was written. A steep path down through the trees below Pike Low brought me on to a lane that runs along the east bank of Ladybower Reservoir towards the

Ashopton village in the late 1920s. This was the old Toll House on the Glossop to Sheffield road. In the background stands a wooden hut and three hand-cranked petrol pumps.

Water cascades over the giant wall of Derwent Reservoir.

For a few years the tower of Derwent Church protruded from the waters of Ladybower Reservoir.
In 1947, however, it was demolished.

sunken village of Derwent. When the guide was published there was an ivy-covered mansion, Derwent Hall, with extensive gardens, a narrow-arched stone bridge over the infant river, a vicarage, a steepled church, a village school and several farms.

Derwent Hall, complete with oak-panelled rooms, fine tapestries and its own chapel, was an attractive rambling building, the date 1672 carved over the main doorway at the head of a flight of stone steps. The Duke of Norfolk used it as a base for shooting forays on the 2,000 acres of moorland he owned. Sometimes walkers would meet the Duke tramping along the lane in well-worn tweeds.

There is a reliable story that the Duke, and his equally-energetic Duchess, climbed Win Hill one summer's day in the 1920s, mistakenly took a wrong track, crossed a field and climbed over a wall. The farmer at Cox Bridge Farm mistook them for hikers and berated them. The Duke, who apologised but did not reveal his identity, sent a cheque to the farmer the following day in recompense.

In 1932 Derwent Hall was opened by the Prince of Wales as a youth hostel. During the Second World War it housed evacuees from a Sheffield school, but in 1973 it was demolished with much of the rest of the village.

The packhorse bridge was carefully dismantled stone by stone, and some years later, re-erected at Slippery Stones high up.the valley, in memory of John Derry, a Sheffield walker who did much to publicise lesser known paths over the Peak District hills.

After the flooding, only the church tower and steeple were left standing, and for some years they were a popular landmark protruding from the water. In 1947 they too were demolished. The four bells that once hung in the tower can still be heard, however -in the church at Chelmorton on the moors high above Buxton.

The walk along the eastern side of the Derwent valley was pleasantly graded for me. A kestrel hovered over the pines. A group of brightly-clad walkers passed me and I remembered the homily given by the Heywood guide: *"Young men (no mention of women, I noticed) whose usual pursuits are sedentary are advised when taking a holiday tour amidst mountain scenery to keep within their strength, especially for the first two or three days."*

With the sun turning the long bracken-covered slope below Whinstone Lee Tor a burnished gold, I regained the A57 near Ladybower Bridge and returned the guide to my pocket.

We have lost a lot by the flooding of this picturesque valley, but so much more of the countryside has been made available to the walker that the area is still one of the most exhilarating in the entire Peak.

Errwood Reservoir in the Goyt Valley is bordered by stately Scots pine trees.
A six-pound trout was caught here in 1973.

The placid River Dove in Beresford Dale.  A wooden footbridge crosses the stream at this point.

Chapter Eight
# THE GIANT RAINBOWS

The high moors are not the only features of the Peak that appeal to lovers of the countryside. Rivers that meander through luxuriant meadows, such as the delightful and slow-moving Wye at Bakewell and Monsal Dale, have attracted both walkers and anglers for more than 200 years.

Every day during the main tourist season people can be seen leaning over the parapet of Bakewell's medieval stone-arched bridge, watching trout darting among trailing green weeds. It is a scene that has not changed for centuries, despite the threat imposed by traffic crossing the river at this narrow point.

When that intrepid Victorian traveller I mentioned earlier, Edward Bradbury, leaned over this same Bakewell Bridge wall in the 19th century he *"chatted about trout"* with anglers and claimed to have seen one of them catch an immense eight-pounder.

It is questionable that any eight-pounders are in the river today - two pounders are now considered good catches. In 1900, in the Rutland estate office at Bakewell, there was a fine five and a quarter pound trout on display in a glass case. Others weighing almost three pounds in weight have been caught in recent years - one by Laurie Williamson beneath Milford Cottage Bridge in 1992. But no one has caught anything approaching eight pounds.

To catch an eight-pounder these days anglers have to fish in a lake or a pool at a trout hatchery. However a six pound rainbow trout was caught by a Buxton man fly-fishing in the Errwood Reservoir in June 1973, and the biggest catch recorded in recent years in Derbyshire was at Ladybower Reservoir in April 1993 when an incredible 16-pound rainbow was landed, after a half hour struggle, by 74 year-old William Halstead of Bakewell

It is Derbyshire's rivers, however, that have always offered superb sport to anglers. I once stood on a narrow wooden footbridge over the River Wye near Bakewell and talked with David Crossland of the Haddon Estate, which owns fishing rights on a seven-mile stretch of the river. Mr Crossland watched

A fly-fisherman kneels at the side of the River Dove near Milldale and casts a Greenwell's Glory over the water.

a fly-fisherman casting for trout in a wide, pebbly pool a few yards further upstream. I told him that Louis Jennings, who wrote about Derbyshire in 1880, had commented that most trout in the Wye near Bakewell had been removed by enthusiastic fishermen by day and impoverished poachers by night. I added that, in 1930, the angling writer Nelson Bromley claimed that grayling, another tasty game fish, had completely vanished from the river.

But David Crossland dismissed such tales: *"This river is full of big fat rainbow trout and many grayling"*, he said. As we talked the angler in the pool hooked a handsome brown trout weighing about a pound. *"See what I mean,"* said David with a grin.

The traveller, William Worcestre, wrote about the Wye as long ago as the fifteenth century. The river contained *"good salmon"* he said. But salmon vanished from Derbyshire's rivers at the end of the last century due to increasing pollution in the River Trent. In 1881 only three were caught in the lower reaches of the River Dove, although many salmon were still reported spawning on gravel beds near Willington and Hilton in south Derbyshire.

There were *"fine trouts and eels"* in the tiny Black Brook at Chapel-en-le-Frith in 1751. James Clegg, the preacher and doctor who lived at Stodhart Hall, fished the stream which ran through his grounds, one June afternoon and caught *"almost 10 lbs."* Clegg, who had turned 70, also fished the Wye at Ashford-in-the-Water after preaching at Chatsworth.

A hundred years later angling parties were casting their rods over the river near the old Sheepwash Bridge in the village. They often stayed at the Devonshire Arms where the owner, Mrs Fanny Frost, issued permits. Even today holidaymakers lean over the bridge parapet to gaze at large dark-green trout stemming the current below.

Higher up the Wye, at Millers Dale, the writer William Adam observed *"half a-dozen rods actively employed"* in the 1840s. Around this time poachers were also active in the Wye. The owner of Wormhill Hall, Mr W.H. Bagshawe, died of injuries sustained in a midnight scuffle with poachers on the banks of the river near Millers Dale bridge. Five men were tried for murder but were acquitted - on the plea that the young squire had started the fight.

The River Lathkill near Youlgreave has long been renowned for its fishing. In

Charles Cotton's fishing house which has stood at the side of the River Dove near Hartington since 1674. Cotton lived at Beresford Hall

the 17th century, Charles Cotton described it as *"the purest and most transparent stream that I ever saw"*. Cotton and his friend Isaak Walton were also ecstatic about the River Dove. Almost hidden in the trees on the banks of the Dove near Hartington, Cotton's fishing house still stands and is a tangible link with Walton's classic book *The Compleat Angler.*

A well-known character, who stalked the banks of the Dove near the fishing house for many years, was the remarkable Miss Dora Oliver, the only professional woman river keeper in Britain until she retired a few years ago. I first met her when fly-fishing on the Dove. She bore down on me, accompanied by a fierce-looking dog, waved her walking stick and carefully checked my permit  She knew just where the best trout were lying and said she walked her three-mile beat through Beresford Dale every day. Many anglers now miss her friendly advice and contagious sense of humour.

Some enjoyable fly-fishing can be found in Derbyshire's smaller streams. One or two of these narrow, tree-shaded waterways have vanished due to the building of reservoirs in the early 1900s.  When Walter Gallichan cast dry-flies over the upper reaches of the Derwent in 1903 the Ashopton Inn had not yet been immersed in the depths of Ladybower Reservoir. *"Three miles of trout water are open to visitors at half-a-crown a day"*, he wrote. The inn provided *"a good cook, a bathroom with hot water and plenty of stabling."*

It now costs £60 a day to fish for trout in the Wye at Bakewell or Rowsley during the high season.  When Walter Gallichan roamed these waterside meadows it cost three shillings!

Visitors to Ashford-in-the-Water lean over the parapet of Sheepwash Bridge to watch trout stemming the current of the Wye.

Anglers often visit the pool that lies below this bridge over the River Wye at Upperdale.

A rippling pool on the Wye near Haddon Hall.
Here the author and other anglers have hooked hefty rainbow trout.

## Chapter Nine
# TASTE OF THE PEAK

Trout caught in the River Wye are often on the menu at hotels and restaurants in the Peak today, although few diners would expect to suffer the experience of James Clegg, an eminent Derbyshire clergyman, who got a fish hook in his mouth while eating a meal of poached trout at the Red Lion in Bakewell in 1750.

The standard of food served in the Peak has usually been highly renowned. The Honourable John Byng, for example, tucked into his dinner in the flickering yellow light of an oil lamp one evening in 1790 and expressed himself well satisfied at a Peak District tavern. On the table was *"a quarter of cold lamb, a cold duck, salad, tarts and jelly"* - all for a shilling.

Mr Byng, who later would become the fifth Viscount Torrington, also drank wine, rum and brandy costing him a further 1s 3d, and lashed out fivepence on hay and corn for his horse, before climbing the creaking stairs to his bed.

The tavern was the Rutland Arms Hotel, then known as the White Horse Inn, in the centre of Bakewell. What Byng consumed was typical of the fare served to travellers on their way through the Peak in the 18th century.

The Rutland Arms at Bakewell. It was known as the White Horse Inn when John Byng dined there in 1780.

Not everyone was pleased, however. That renowned author, Celia Fiennes, who travelled extensively across Britain earlier in the 18th century, was not over-impressed with the Hall, Buxton's largest hotel at that time. *"The beer they allow at its meals is so bad that very little can be drunk,'"* she wrote. What is more, the place was so crowded that three people had to squeeze into one bed.

In the previous century conditions had apparently been rather better. The

The Crescent at Buxton today.
Here, in the eastern wing, the Great Hotel's dinner bell rang each day at 3.30 pm.

philosopher Thomas Hobbes, travelling through Derbyshire and staying at the same inn, enjoyed his dinner cooked on a turf fire while guests refreshed their *'tired limbs'* in the adjoining bath. They then sat down to mutton broth, loin of mutton *"smoking from the spit"*, chicken and buttered pies. This was all washed down with *"black flagons of smiling beer"*.

In the 19th century the main meal of the day was served early at the Great Hotel, which stood in the eastern wing of the Crescent at Buxton. *"Our dinner bell rang at 3.30pm",'* wrote Anna Seward in 1808. Among her companions sitting down one afternoon were the Marquis of Hartington, Lord and Lady Shaftesbury and their *"pretty fairy"* daughter, the 18 year old Lady Barbara.

Travel writer James Croston was unhappy when he called at the Red Lion in the village of Birchover in 1870 and noticed an uncovered drain and stagnant pool close to the inn door. The menu was limited but, sitting himself comfortably on a settle in the chimney nook, he nevertheless enjoyed the landlord's *"simple fare"*.

The Red Lion at Birchover. Victorian travellers enjoyed "simple fare" at this ancient inn.

A few miles away, at Hartington, Croston stayed overnight at the Sleigh Arms. Here he enjoyed *"fresh-laid eggs, equally fresh butter and thick clotted cream"* for breakfast and he ate *"with relish"*.

Travellers staying at the New Bath Hotel in Matlock Bath in 1802 were charged threepence for breakfast, two shillings for dinner *"at the public table"* and one shilling for tea. A hundred years later it still cost two shillings for dinner at the Royal Hotel in Hayfield.

By and large travellers who made their way along the Peak's rough roads years ago appear to have been satisfied with the fare and accommodation provided at local hostelries. Charles Moritz, a young Prussian clergyman touring Britain in 1782, and walking through Derbyshire, was directed to the George Hotel near the village church

The New Bath Hotel at Matlock Bath which contains a natural warm water pool below the lounge bar. Breakfast cost 3d in 1802.

Below:
The George Hotel in Tideswell. It stands next to the handsome parish church that is sometimes called "the Cathedral of the Peak".

in Tideswell. He was accommodated *"most magnificently"* and served with *"Cheshire cheese roasted and half melted by the fire"*. The following morning the George's landlady drank coffee with him before he went on his way to Castleton.

As recently as 1920, Nelson Bromley, a keen fly-fisherman, spent two nights at the Granby Croft in Bakewell. For breakfast the *"two good ladies"* who kept the guest house served him with *"delicious rainbow trout"* which had been caught in the nearby River Wye that morning. There were, however, occurrences that were regrettable. The traveller, Arthur Young, staying in 1790 at the Bunch of Grapes, a hostelry in Edensor that vanished long ago, found *"only dirt and impertinence"*. Dr Samuel Johnson, who visited the same tavern four years later, described it as *"a bad inn"*.

But the most crushing observation of Derbyshire fare in the 17th century must go to medical student Edward Browne, who complained that dinner at his lodgings in Buxton - he did not name the tavern - consisted of nothing but *"oatcakes and mutton, which we fancied to taste like dog"*.

This would be an odious libel if applied to Buxton's hotels, and the many inns throughout rural Derbyshire, that dispense most satisfying meals to the hungry visitors and travellers of today.

Chapter Ten
# THE STONE GANGS

Many of the walkers who amble through the fields of the Blackbrook Valley between Chapel-en-1e-Frith and Buxworth today might find it difficult to believe that the silence of these sweet meadows and shady lanes was once broken by the clattering and banging of iron trucks that jolted and clanged along a tramway laid alongside the stream.

It is just 75 years since the last wagons of the Peak Forest Tramway ran through the heart of the High Peak. Now much of the route, along which hundreds of tons of limestone were once transported daily from the quarries of Dove Holes to the canal at Buxworth and onwards to the towns of Lancashire, has been obliterated by new roads and industrial sites, but it is still possible to walk along parts of it in the shade of birch trees and leafy sycamores.

'Gangs' of perhaps 20 iron trucks, piled high with rough limestone, ran by gravity for six miles from the quarries in the hills, a brakeman and a boy assistant (known as a 'nipper') perched precariously on the leading wagon.

After the trucks were emptied into waiting barges at Buxworth, they were hauled back up the line by strings of horses, many hired from local farmers. Sam and Herbert Green used their two heavy horses, Flower and Turpin, to haul trucks between the canal and their stables at Chapel-en-le-Frith. Noah Berrisford worked as a horseman for 30 years until 1920 on the section between Chapel and Dove Holes.

The canal basin at Buxworth in 1910. This was where the Peak Forest Tramway terminated.
Loads of limestone from the Dove Holes quarries were tipped into waiting barges.

A typical scene on a tramway at the end of the 19th Century.

Stone sleepers to which the tramway rails were secured are on display in the restored basin at Buxworth today.

Noah, who lived at Wibbersley Farm, Dove Holes, was in charge of three horses and worked seven days a week, being paid about £1 a week by the quarry owners. *"I remember how the harness jingled when I walked the horses down the track,"* he told me. *"But it sometimes needed five horses to pull the empty trucks up from Top o' th' Plane."* Luckily, there were several stone water troughs along the line to quench the horses' thirst.

No passengers were carried on the tramway but Noah remembered seeing company officials wearing black overcoats and bowler hats sitting bolt upright in a special horse-drawn truck during one of their tours of inspection.

The tramway was built by the engineer, Benjamin Outram, in the 1790s. He had constructed a canal from Ashton-under-Lyne to Buxworth (then called Bugsworth) and intended to extend it to Chapel Milton which was only four miles from the quarries. But the cost of constructing several locks and a large reservoir in the nearby Wash valley, to supply a sufficient head of water, proved too costly, and the rails of his planned tramway were laid along the Black Brook valley from Buxworth instead.

The line, which opened in 1797, was an instant success. As many as 20 barges, each holding 20 tons of limestone, left Buxworth Basin each day for Lancashire.

At Loads Knowl, where the first quarries in Dove Holes Dale were located and where high quality limestone was extracted, the 'gangs' of trucks were pushed off down the track. They gathered speed under the present A6 road near Dove Holes village and down through the woods of Barmoor Clough, the line protected on either side by drystone walls.

The 'gangs' came to a halt at Top o'th' Plane, a flattened area of sidings and workshops at the end of a 900-ft high ridge overlooking the houses of Chapel-en-le-Frith. Here the brakeman and his 'nipper' thrust iron 'sprags' through the spokes of the wagon wheels before the 'gang' was lowered down a 500-yard 1-in-7 inclined plane worked by a two-inch-thick wire rope and counter-balanced by a string of empty trucks coming up the gradient at the same time.

The old smithy and workshops at Top o'th' Plane still stand but have been converted in recent years into handsome country homes. At the foot of the slope, where the track again ran under the A6, the 'gangs' were re-marshalled and pushed off again on the next stage of their journey. Soon they were clattering across Bowden Lane and through a copse of oak and elm where Ferodo workers now park their cars.

A mile beyond Chapel-en-le-Frith stood Stodhart Tunnel, 100 yards long and entered through a steep-sided cutting, the slopes of which were covered with ivy and rhododendron bushes. Then the 'gang' hurtled through Chapel Milton and past the former Spread Eagle Inn - there were sidings here where two or three wagons of lime might be shunted off for local farmers - before winding through the pleasant fields of Bridgholm and along the banks of the Black Brook to Buxworth.

There were extensive sidings at Buxworth and much of the limestone was tipped into large storage bays at the canalside below the level of the track. Wagons were pushed into a 16-ft high tipping wheel which spun round and deposited the cargoes of limestone into the capacious holds of barges waiting in the basin.

In addition to the bulk transport of limestone the 'gangs' also carried pure lime that had been refined in smoke-shrouded kilns at the quarries. In 1848 a notice was posted on the Buxworth wharf stating that Buxton lime could be loaded into carts *"in 15 minutes after it arrives at 7s 1d per ton and put into boats at 7s 6d per ton."*

My father remembered playing on the tramway a few years before it ceased operations in 1923. *"There were frequent derailments,"* he told me. *"When we came across a discarded truck or one left in the Spread Eagle sidings we would push it down the track until one of the brakemen chased us off."*

Unlike railway tracks, the tramway rails were L-shaped and they sat on square stone sleepers, secured by iron spikes driven into oak plugs inserted inside the sleepers. The clatter of the 'gangs', their iron wheels grinding against the raised flanges and banging over primitive joints linking the 9-ft long rails, must have been horrendous. There were cobbles between the rails that enabled horses to obtain a firm grip.

At one time there were plans to extend the tramway to Buxton and to build a spur line to Sparrowpit and possibly over the Rushup moors to Ashopton, but the introduction of railways in the early days of Queen Victoria's reign soon began to interfere with the slower canal and tramway traffic. When the London and North Eastern Railway took over the Peak Forest Tramway in 1923 the rails were uprooted and the 'gangs' of trucks scrapped, although one wagon can still be seen in the National Railway Museum at York.

The building of this historic old tramway had fascinated the villagers of the High Peak at the end of the 18th century. Mrs Grace Bennett, an evangelist and friend of John Wesley, wrote in 1795: *'I took a walk* (from her home at Stodhart) *to Barmoor Clough to see the railway they are making. I thought it would be very dangerous."'*

In a further observation, which well illustrates the social conditions of those distant days, Mrs Bennett wrote: *"On my return I met a poor woman without shoes. I spoke to her. She told me she had walked from Manchester that day and was going to Sheffield in quest of her husband who had 'gone away with the soldiers.'"*

Early in this century one of the best-known men employed as a ganger on the tramway was Jack Eyre, a bright-eyed man with a drooping moustache who lived in a small house alongside the track near the Forge Mill at Chinley. My grandfather recalled the evenings when a 'gang' would stop for the night outside Jack's house, the wheels being secured with several 'sprags'. At first light the following morning the 'sprags' would be removed and Jack would send the trucks on their way to Buxworth.

Little of the old tramway is now open to walkers, although the section from Dove Holes to the top of Barmoor Clough and part of the route near Top o' th' Plane can still be explored. Unfortunately, one of the most scenic sections of the line, from Chapel Milton to Bridgholm, was taken over by Ferodo Ltd many years ago and covered in tarmac so that the company's drivers could test clutch and brake linings in high speed cars.

The canal basin during restoration.
In the background is the Navigation Inn which is full of canal memorabilia.

Since 1968 volunteers have been working to renovate the basin at Buxworth - it is intended to attract pleasure boats into a marina - and much of the area has been restored to its original appearance.

Limestone is still carried into Lancashire and Cheshire, from the North Derbyshire quarries by rail, and increasingly by road. Trains loaded with 1,000 tons of stone travel continuously to a large chemical plant at Northwich and other destinations. The tramway 'gangs' carried about 50 tons at a time. Benjamin Outram would have scratched his head in disbelief.

Wedding day in 1893. George Hewitt and his bride Cissie Walker walk to church under
Chapel Milton's railway arches - a picture from Alfred's album.

Upper Fold Farm, in a valley below South Head, photographed by Alfred Clowes.
Here he met his bride Elizabeth Simpson.

## Chapter Eleven
# ALFRED'S CAMERA

The trucks of the Peak Forest Tramway were still rattling past the old Spread Eagle Inn, at Chapel Milton, when Alfred Clowes, one of the few men in the district to possess a camera, climbed to the side of the track with a heavy tripod and looked down on the hamlet as it prepared to celebrate King Edward VII's Coronation in 1901.

Village elders travel in a horse-drawn dray under a garlanded arch at Chapel Milton on Coronation Day 1901.
One of Alfred's favourite photographs.

A procession under the great railway arches, that loom over the village roofs to this day, had been planned for weeks. Alfred was ready. He crouched under a black focusing cloth, swiftly inserted a glass plate into a wooden slide holder and squeezed the rubber ball of the camera's pneumatic shutter.

Albert had paid £2 for his 'Instantograph' half-plate camera with its smart brass lens mount, leather bellows and polished wooden base. *"I set out to photograph the subjects around me,"* he said many years later. *"Then I would hurry home to develop the plates in the stone sink in our blacked-out kitchen."* Luckily, the old leather-bound album in which he carefully pasted his beautiful sepia prints is still in existence.

Walking in the hills around Chapel Milton occupied much of Alfred's spare time - he was employed as a signalman by the Midland Railway and it was when

Strawboaters in the Wash hamlet in the 1890s.
Two neighbours pose for Alfred's camera at the side of the Cornheys stream.

passing remote Upper Fold Farm, not far from his home, that he met 19-year-old Anne Elizabeth Simpson. Twelve months later she became his bride.

Alfred took pleasure in photographing local scenes, but he was often in demand to 'snap' the inhabitants of Chapel Milton. They would pose in Alfred's small Victorian parlour, or against a plain white sheet stretched over the back door of the terraced cottage.

The women held diaphanous scarves in their hands and wore wide floral hats. White embroidered collars covered their shoulders, their waists tightly belted and their long tailored skirts draped over neat pointed shoes. A kitchen table almost buried under a large sheepskin rug frequently featured in his 'studio' shots.

Alfred was a tall man with receding hair and a small moustache. He often wore a cravat under a high-lapelled jacket with a single Albert watch chain looped across his waistcoat. A carnation was usually in his buttonhole.

*"There were no other photographers in Chapel Milton. I took pictures - always using a heavy tripod - of many local farms and manor houses, and all of my friends. Family groups would sometimes pose for me, and when the Chapel Milton Sunday School held a concert I would photograph the chorus girls in the field behind my house."*

Alfred was often accompanied by his friend, a solicitor's clerk named George

Barrett, who came in very handy when the tripod, camera and heavy box of glass plates had to be lugged around. *"After using the Instantograph for a few years I bought a bulky secondhand Newman and Guardia camera with a detachable changing box for plates and films, but that was even heavier."*

Photography was still in its infancy when Alfred, his wife and a young daughter, moved to the hamlet of Two Dales for a couple of years. Soon he was asked to take pictures at Stancliffe Quarries in Darley Dale and the railway goods sidings at Rowsley. Stancliffe Quarries were owned by Sir Joseph Whitworth, a brilliant but somewhat eccentric engineer who lived at Stancliffe Hall and was a pioneer of precision tool-making and rifle-barrelled guns.

In the stone yard at the quarries as many as 40 masons chiselled and shaped the much-prized pure pink gritstone that was hewn from the hillside above Darley Dale. The flagstones of Trafalgar Square and the Thames Embankment came from the quarry and the stones were also used for Chatsworth House, and the Walker Art Gallery and St Georges Hall in Liverpool - in the latter case being carried by pack pony to Cromford and despatched across country by canal boat.

By the time Alfred died, in 1958, photography had become a worldwide hobby, yet he still kept that old Instantograph camera in his sitting room. His many valuable glass negatives did not survive, however - his grandsons used them as targets for their airguns.

Local farmers pose for Alfred on a summer's day in 1897.

A prominent gritstone crag on the escarpment near Roach End.

Weathered crags, splintered and cracked, are characteristic of the Roaches where wallabies once roamed.

## Chapter Twelve
# OUT OF BOUNDS

I recall a beautiful summer's day in the 1980s when I was scanning with my binoculars the wild heather moorland on the Roaches, those remarkable splintered rocks between Buxton and Leek.

*"I suppose you're trying to see a wallaby,"* said Len Page, the local Peak Park warden, when he joined me in the shade of Bearstone Rock.

He was right. l had visited the Roaches, a dramatic craggy gritstone ridge at the south west corner of the Peak District National Park, on many occasions - in all weathers and all seasons - each time hoping, in vain, for a sight of the elusive wild wallabies.

The Roaches lie in Staffordshire and their jagged pinnacles of rock and steep slopes of grass, heather and bilberry are far removed from the dry plains of Australia where the bounding wallabies are normally to be found.

The Roaches in North Staffordshire where wallabies lived for many years.
Hen Cloud (1,240 feet) is on the right.

The furry marsupials, little larger than mountain hares and like small kangaroos, were descendants of animals kept in a private zoo at Swythamley Hall in the 1930s. When their owner, Colonel Brocklehurst, allowed them to escape at the start of the Second World War, they established themselves on the nearby Roaches, thriving on young bracken, bilberry shoots and grass. Despite successive severe winters they bred and increased in numbers. At one time the colony was nearly 50 strong.

They are shy creatures, although Len Page frequently saw them as he walked the Swythamley Estate. *"Just their little heads among the heather"*, he said. *"Particularly when it was the grouse-shooting season. The guns sure kept them on their toes."*

Walkers on the heather and rock moor that covers the Roaches.

By 1976, naturalists from Manchester University believed that only about 20 were left. Three were killed that year by cars on the narrow unfenced road that crosses the moor, and the long and bitterly-cold winters in the years shortly after then put increasing pressure on the animals. In August 1978 a young male wallaby from Riber Hall Wildlife Park, near Matlock, was released on the Roaches and, despite a harsh snowbound winter in early 1979, observers counted about 20 animals, including the new male, the following spring.

Len Page came across an old, emaciated wallaby lying on the moor not far from Roach End in January 1996 and took it in his Land Rover to be treated by a vet in Leek. But the animal soon died.

Dr Derek Yalden, of Manchester University, saw his first wallaby in 1967 and has studied them ever since. *"They are now certainly extinct on the Roaches."* he confirmed. *"Their numbers dwindled rapidly over the past five years. They are hardy animals, known to live to 20 years in Australia. I watched one female on the Roaches for 13 years at least."*

Inquisitive sightseers and inevitable old age probably affected the animals' breeding behaviour. Unfortunately,the bleak winters in the late 1970s and a regrettable mortality rate among the breeding males, especially from car accidents, finally wiped out the colony. Sightings of individual animals were reported until 1996, although there are still rumours about their existence.

No one can really explain why they survived for so long on the exposed moor - especially through the very harsh winter of 1947. The windswept Roaches are now left to red grouse and meadow pipits. The mystery of why they lived so long amid the rocks and clumps of heather in this harsh Pennine landscape will probably never he solved.

Chapter Thirteen
# THE TUNNEL LINE

Since the arrival of the railway age at the beginning of the 19th century, railway lines have inevitably tunnelled their way through the hills that separate the cities of Manchester and Sheffield. The first was built in 1845 and the last nearly 50 years later - the 15-mile Hope Valley line that still remains one of the most secluded and beautiful lines in the country.

It took six years to lay rails through the Hope Valley, mainly due to the problems of tunnelling under the moors at either end of the vale. In fact, a quarter of the route between Dore and Chinley is underground to this day.

Edward Bradbury, spending an *"idle, careless time fishing, sketching and shooting"* in the Derwent valley in 1883, wrote: *"One devoutly hopes that the projected railway which is to give Sheffield a new route to Manchester will never break the seclusion of so much sealed charm."* If Bradbury were alive today I think he would see that his fears were luckily unfounded. The line has done little harm to the Hope Valley as it carries express trains from one side of Britain to the other.

Although the line opened in 1893 it was not until the following year that stations inside the valley were completed and a local passenger service started. Brass bands met passengers at Hope, flags flew all along the line and there were free trips to Edale and back for children in Hathersage.

Many years ago Mr Ollerenshaw, formerly of North Lees Hall, Hathersage, well remembered the occasion. He had hoped very much to travel on one of the special trains but his mother would not let him go *"because it was too dangerous."*

The 34 mile long tunnel between Dore and Totley and a new station at Grindleford caused most difficulties for the contractors. The Duke of Rutland objected to ventilation shafts on the moors as *"game would be frightened by the smoke"*, and when tunnelling eventually started water began to flood the workings, sometimes being pumped out at the rate of 5,000 gallons a minute. A newspaper reporter who visited the scene wrote: *"Every man seemed to be possessed of the miraculous power of Moses - whenever he struck a rock water sprang out of it."*

At the western end of the Hope Valley scores of navvies dug under the Cowburn moors. A massive ventilation shaft was sunk 800 feet to the track below. In the days of steam there was a constant plume of white smoke hanging over the stone shaft, which is still plainly visible to motorists crossing Rushup Edge.

Cowburn Tunnel is more than two miles long. It is dead straight, its brick lining reinforced with strong iron hoops. Local farmers provided horses and carts to carry spoil to a large tip at Chapel Milton - the great heap of shale and sandstone

Cattle graze across the valley from Grindslow Knoll. The railway lies just beyond the central line of trees.

A Midland Railway train emerges from Dore and Totley Tunnel at Grindleford,
soon after the line was opened in 1894.

is now covered in grass and maintained as a nature reserve - and many navvies lived in crude, overcrowded and insanitary huts. Some were accommodated in the Chinley Chapel sunday school, the trustees allocating 15 shillings for coal and 6d per month for *"uplifting"* magazines such as *The British Worker* and the *Artisan Band of Hope.*

A works' locomotive was manhandled into the valley over the high Rushup Edge road from Chapel-en-le-Frith Station to Edale to assist the tunnellers. An old man once told the Derbyshire historian, Crichton Porteous, how the engine was *"leap-frogged"* along the road, a team of horses towing a short length of track on a low-loader and the engine moving upwards in short bursts of steam.

Fifteen new locomotives were built at Derby for the opening of the line and it is interesting to note that the first passenger trains from Sheffield to Manchester (making only one stop at Marple) took 1 hour 20 minutes for the journey. Forty years later, calling at four intermediate stations, the fastest trains took 1 hour 15 minutes. Nowadays non-stop expresses complete the trip in just 53 minutes.

Accidents on the Hope Valley line have been few, probably due to the virtual absence of junctions along the route. The most destructive was a head-on collision at Hope in 1925 caused-by a signalman who, forgetting that a ballast train was already standing on the line, gave a green signal to a Manchester-Sheffield express. The express's driver and fireman were killed but by great good fortune only one passenger was hurt.

The track and signalling arrangements have been modernised in recent years - the old signalbox at Bamford now stands at Peak Rail's new station in Darley Dale - and smoke from steam trains no longer threatens to disturb the grouse on Totley Moor.

My thoughts have often turned to the old stone-roofed barn where my pals and I met to play cowboys and indians in the 1930s. It had one great advantage; it overlooked the London, Midland and Scottish Railway's main line through the Peak.

We would often put aside our pistols and tomahawks and sit at the

A modern day train on the Hope Valley line speeds down from the western end of Cowburn Tunnel. A footpath that crosses the line here is known as the "Forty Steps".

little hayloading door that pierced the wall of the barn's dusty loft to watch trains snorting up the incline from Chinley station.

Halfway down the heather-cloaked slope of a cutting between two bridges we found a convenient rock shelter that was almost a cave. In here we built camp fires. Avoiding the eagle eye of patrolling ganger Sam Waterhouse, we crouched as close as we could to locomotives grinding past at the head of 40 or more wagons, taking care to duck down when the guard's van came into view.

My brother and I were particularly delighted when a "Little Buxton" puffed up the line. This was the regular local passenger train that ran backwards and forwards several times a day between Buxton and Chinley, enabling passengers from the spa town to catch connections for stations on the Sheffield line. More important was that the locomotive was sometimes driven by our Uncle Tom. On catching sight of us he would wave cheerily from his cab and toot his whistle. That really made our day.

Tom Harrison was born in Middleton, near Wirksworth, just before the end of Queen Victoria's reign and married Hannah Doxey, a pretty girl who lived across the road from him, at Holy Trinity Parish Church in 1916 while on leave from the Front in France. The best man was Tom's elder brother Joe, a wild character who had emigrated some years before and was now serving in the Australian Army. There was also Tom's brother Jack. My mother, then a schoolgirl, was a bridesmaid.

When the war ended in 1918 Uncle Tom - actually, my great uncle - joined the Midland Railway and moved to Buxton to work as a cleaner in the engine sheds off Bridge Street. He and Hannah lived in a terraced house overlooking Ashwood Dale, and before very long they started a family. A boy and two girls were born to them.

Cleaning steam locomotives was the first stage of an engine driver's career. An arduous and dirty job it was, too. It usually took six lads to clean one engine. Tom started work at midnight and went home around 8.00am. He helped to shunt locomotives around the shed's network of lines, got coal into the tenders and, worst of all, scraped ash and clinker from under the fireboxes. *"My overalls were soon coated in ash and char,"* remembered Tom. *"I was blackened from head to foot."*

In the 1930s the Midland sheds at Buxton were closed and new ones built. Tom began working as a fireman on goods trains heading down Chee Dale and through Chinley to the extensive sidings at Gowhole near New Mills. *"I had to keep the fire dancing on the bars,"* he told me. *"Two shovelfuls of coal down the front of the firebox, two down each side, and one occasionally under the doors."*

Sometimes the engine on which he worked had to travel tender-first through Peak District gales. *"There was no tarpaulin sheet to protect us from the weather,"* he said. *No wonder I had ruddy cheeks when I got home."*

During the war years, Tom became a regular driver, first on goods trains, then on local passenger services. The "Little Buxton" duty was one of his favourites. It was downhill most of the way from Buxton, around the squealing curve at Blackwell Hill, past the sprawling ICI quarry in Great Rocks Dale to Peak Forest, through the damp, dark, two mile long Dove Holes tunnel, a stop at Chapel-en-le-Frith and then on over high viaducts at Chapel Milton to reach the major junction station at Chinley.

If the signals were in his favour, the journey took 25 minutes, but the pull back to Buxton took 10 minutes more. In fact the climb was known to all enginemen as the Chinley Bank, or sometimes, the Steep Drag.

Uncle Tom's trains usually consisted of only three coaches. Longer trains found the final three mile climb from Chapel-en-le-Frith to the 985-ft summit at Peak Forest particularly difficult. Drivers and firemen, in the open cabs of goods engines, often found Dove Holes Tunnel quite diabolical, forcing them to crouch or even kneel as acrid sulphurous smoke enveloped the footplate.

The 'Peak Express' and the 'Palatine' were the only express trains carrying names. The sight of engines, called *Jellicoe* or *Leeward Islands*, roaring up the gradient, a low sun gleaming on their red boilers and tenders, steam spurting around the whirring wheels and long ribbons of white smoke drifting towards the bracken-covered slopes of Eccles Pike, was a spectacle that I can still vividly recall today.

Unfortunately, locomotives were not maintained to the same high standards after the war. By then I had grown up a little and no longer climbed into the old barn. Instead, I leaned on the smoke-blackened parapet of Dakins Bridge, still watching the emotive trains go by. Only a few years remained before steam locomotives climbed the Chinley Bank for the last time and colourless diesels took their place.

The London-bound Palatine Express steams up the Chinley Bank in 1960.
Nearby is the trackside barn where driver Tom Harrison waved to his nephews.

The Winnats Pass near Castleton today.  The first of several demonstrations
to gain access to the moors was held here in 1928.

The masthead of *Out-o'-Doors* magazine in May 1928.

## Chapter Fourteen
# PLUS FOURS ON THE MOORS

It is a long time since residents of the Peak District looked on ramblers as mad enthusiasts clad in long khaki shorts and hob-nailed boots. But this seems to have been the case in the 1920s according to the pages of a long-forgotten outdoor magazine.

I was intrigued when I came across a battered copy of *Out-o'-Doors* - described as *"the mag. for every lover of the open air"* -amid a nondescript pile of grubby Western paperbacks and well-thumbed woodwork manuals, on the bottom shelf of a second-hand bookshop in a Derbyshire village. The edges of its pages were turning brown with age, its photographic illustrations were blurred and its advertisements liberally laced with quaint old-fashioned drawings. In 1928 the ramblers' *"Own Monthly"* was popular among walkers and cyclists throughout the country. It cost 3d.

The magazine's columnist "Old Campaigner" criticises cottagers for looking upon ramblers as *"mad"*. *"Only occasionally"*, he comments, *"can an inn be found where the landlady can be persuaded to make a pot of tea"*. How different from today.

The Peak District is featured throughout the magazine. A letter to the editor from a Stockport woman thanks three ramblers who carried her on their backs when she sprained her ankle badly near Jacob's Ladder on the Kinder moors. Mr Bennett, a local farmer, also came to her rescue, providing a horse to transport her to Hayfield Station.

Another letter writer objects to the word "rambler" and prefers that genuine country walkers should be called *"wanderbirds"*. He also feels that the word *"bogtrotter"* is *"forbidding to gentlemen in collars and plus-fours"*.

Edgar Morton, a professional geologist from Manchester University, offers a Saturday afternoon excursion to the caves of Castleton for one shilling a head and the Rev. Frederick Bent, vicar of Peak Forest, invites ramblers to his church's *"open house"* on Sunday afternoons - events that readers are assured are *"not starchy"* as they include the community singing of such numbers as *Swanee River* and *Pack Up Your Troubles*.

The National Trust's appeal for £14,000 to purchase about 747 acres of the Longshaw Estate near Hathersage is extensively reported in the magazine. We read of volunteer *"Longshaw wardens"* being provided with armlets and collecting tins. During one weekend a party of 12 volunteers widened paths on the moors, collected litter and raised the *"magnificent sum"* of £23 3s 6d for the appeal.

Even at this early date demonstrations to gain access to the moors were taking place. Ramblers are asked to gather in the Winnats Pass at Castleton on June 24th to support the Access to Mountains Bill. The principal speaker was to be Mr C.P. Trevelyan MP.

*Out-o'Doors* includes many small advertisements. Khaki shorts cost 5s each. Plus-fours are popular for both walkers and cyclists, particularly ones with *"wide knee bands for fancy hose"*. Some even have a *"free extra seat"*. It costs 1s a night to camp at Sparks Bottom Farm in Whaley Bridge and tea rooms, with accommodation for 60, are available at Mrs Smith's establishment in the now-submerged village of Derwent.

Mrs Moore of Matlock Bath offers bed and breakfast facilities and boasts the possession of a piano for the use of guests.

So much for the outdoor scene of the 1920s. The world has changed a lot - we seldom see plus-fours today.

Plus-fours for the gentleman walker and a sensible coat for his companion.
This is from an advertisement in the magazine.

Plus-fours and bicycles in the Peak in Edwardian days.

## Chapter Fifteen
# THE APOSTLE'S VALLEY

The two young men I met near Malcoff Farm on the moors between Chapel-en-le-Frith and Edale had never heard of plus-fours.  Nor, in fact, of the secret meetings that were once held little more than a stone's throw from where we stood.

Both lads, stripped to the waist in the warm sunshine, their chests as brown as matured walnut, were eager to complete a 12-mile tramp around 1,866-ft Brown Knoll which lay just out of sight over a shoulder of the moor.

Walkers on the old packhorse trail above Malcoff Farm.
They were unaware of the historic building only a few hundred yards away.

We leaned on a stone gate stump in the shade of a copse of beech trees and looked across the shadowy defile of Roych Clough. After I had explained how many young men in the 1920s and 30s wore plus-fours - baggy trousers buttoned below the knee - they went on their way with grinning faces and my thoughts returned to the history of the barn at Malcoff.

The Reverend William Bagshawe was a wealthy clergyman with an estate at Ford Hall.  His unlawful services in the 17th Century led him to be known as "the Apostle of the Peak".

A law passed in 1662 allowed only one form of religious worship in Britain, and it was against this that Bagshawe rebelled. He was cunning, however. Each Sunday morning he continued to attend the Anglican church at nearby Chapel-en-

The Independent Chapel at Chinley which was built in 1711. Ivy covers its walls.
The minister, Dr James Clegg, complained in 1732 "we had frost and snow and not a full congregation".

Ford Hall, the original home of William Bagshawe, the Apostle of the Peak.

le-Frith, as the law required, but, unknown to the authorities, began to preach in the Non-conformist way at Ford Hall in the evenings.

The Ford Hall servants talked volubly when they went to Chapel market so Bagshawe thought it prudent to switch his followers to Malcoff Farm where his brother-in-law provided him with a barn for use as a chapel. Congregations of 120 or more often attended the secret evening services.

Ford Hall and Malcoff Farm are still situated in a quiet corner of the Derbyshire Peak. Although a turnpike road was built across the boundary of the Ford estate in 1818 and a railway line tunnelled through the valley 80 years later, this tranquil part of the National Park has never been seriously disturbed since the days of the 'Apostle'.

On this warm and sunny day I had decided to walk around the Apostle's secret valley, leaving my car on a side road that leads from the A624 to the tiny hamlet of Wash. First of all, however, I went back along the lane for 200 yards to Chinley Chapel, a two-storey stone building with ivy-covered walls that was erected in 1711. By this time in history the law controlling religious meetings had been eased. Nevertheless, armed guards had to stand over the building workers, shutters were fitted to protect the first small-paned windows, and when the chapel was finally built rotten eggs were hurled by zealous 'high churchmen' at Non-conformist worshippers walking to the chapel on Sunday mornings.

I crossed a small stone bridge at the side of a ford and turned right to follow a lane past the green slab roofs of Slack House Farm which was gay with bright geraniums outside its tiny windows and bore a stone plaque with the date 1762 carved on it. In the yard I met Mr Stanley Drabble who ran a large herd of cattle at Slack House. A faint bellow came from the depths of the barn. *"That's Nuoro,"* said Mr Drabble. He was justly proud of his giant Italian bull which weighed a ton and was thought to be the first Piedmontese to be reared in Britain.

Above the farm an old packhorse trail winds around Mount Famine and South Head and across the high land from Hayfield to Tideswell, the stretch that skirts the Cowburn moors offering some of the finest hill walking in Derbyshire. It is most dramatic when crossing Roych Clough, the walled track here plunging down to a tiny stream, then climbing around the shoulder of Toot Hill to level off above a smooth slope of green fields dropping down towards Malcoff Farm.

After crossing the A625 I stepped over an antique wooden stile and walked along Breck Edge to a triangular-shaped green overlooking the Apostle's old home at Ford Hall. More than 100 years ago a great illegal prize fight was staged at this remote spot, well away from the attention of local police.

The popularity of a pugilist named Bendigo, "the Nottingham Bruiser", attracted a large crowd and the lane was apparently choked with scores of horse-

Eccles Pike seen from the lane that links Malcoff with Ford Hall.

drawn vehicles. Bendigo, a giant six-footer, squared up to Tom Lucy, his challenger, in a rough, roped-off ring at the side of the lane, and won the fight in ten minutes. No one knows how much money the punters won or lost on the fight.

At Slack Hall, an old farmhouse perilously close to the road that descends to Chapel-en-le-Frith, there is a wide-canopied horse chestnut tree that was planted in 1837 to celebrate the Coronation of Queen Victoria.

Just inside a gateway only a few yards from the tree is a small walled enclosure with a tall Douglas fir in one corner. This was where persecuted Quakers buried their dead in the 17th Century. Several tombstones are clearly in view, one bearing the date 1671. The tiny cemetery is now part of the Chestnut Centre, a sanctuary for owls and otters established by architect Roger Heap in the grounds of Ford Hall in the valley below.

The hall, now divided into flats, and its outbuildings now converted into handsome country dwellings, are thought to have been built in the reign of Henry III, but it was in the 1660s that William Bagshawe went to live there. He travelled extensively throughout the Peak District, preaching in many villages, but it was to Ford, in its sylvan valley amid the hills, that he returned each evening. The Apostle's present day descendants left the hall in 1950.

Bagshawe died in 1702 and his successor was the Rev. James Clegg, an indefatigable minister, doctor and farmer who lived at Stodhart near Chapel-en-le-Frith but retained close links with Ford. His diaries reveal something of his busy life in the Derbyshire Peak.

One June evening in 1730 he took his wife on horseback *"to visit Mrs Bagshawe"* at Ford. A few days later he was called to Adam Young at Ford who was *"ill of the measles"*. He also went hare coursing with Mr Bagshaw, *"took some blood"* from Mrs Bagshaw for an undisclosed ailment, and treated her husband for rheumatism with a mixture of gum arabic and camphor. On one wild winter's day his mare plunged into a snowdrift outside Chinley Chapel and *"cast me over her head."*

The horse chestnut tree at Slack Hall, planted to commemorate Queen Victoria's Coronation in 1837.

The barn at Malcoff, where Bagshawe risked imprisonment to hold his prayer meetings, is now an attractive private house, but a stone lintel bearing the date 1702 can still be seen over a doorway.

The lane that leads to the hamlet from Ford Hall is lined today with handsome tall sycamores. Woods still cover Bowden Head, and the cone of Eccles Pike peeps over a cluster of hawthorns and beech trees along the Wash stream. It is a view that has scarcely changed over the centuries and it is little wonder that Bagshawe chose this remote valley for his secret services 300 years ago.

In some ways, the Reverend Willie Simpson of Chinley Chapel in modern days resembled the 17th Century Apostle of the Peak. Instead of a horse this indefatigable clergymen frequently rode a bicycle on the lanes around his chapel but later it was common practice for motorists to give him a helpful lift. I was one of many who were occasionally hi-jacked by this much respected and lovable character. He died in 2003 at the age of 104.

The old barn at Malcoff was used as a secret chapel by Reverend Bagshawe in the 17th Century. It is now a private house.

The rigours of the bleak plateau of Kinder Scout can well be imagined when viewed in winter.

The waters of the infant River Kinder meander down a gorge after falling over the Downfall of Kinder Scout.
It was from rocks below here that a Manchester Boy Scout was rescued in 1957.

## Chapter Sixteen
# PERIL IN THE HILLS

The jagged curtains of millstone grit that slice the green flanks of the Peak District hills, and the heathery bog-scarred moorlands above them, have never failed to lure climbers and walkers from both sides of the Pennines.

But the comparative ease with which young people can reach the rock outcrops, and the increasing rush into the hills each weekend, continues to produce a depressing number of headlines to highlight the hidden perils of the Peak. These hills have always to be respected.

There is nothing really new in the reports we read today of boys trapped on the ledges of Kinder Scout or night-long searches by park rangers and the mountain rescue squads. It was all happening in the 1930s, and the 1940s, and the 1950s.

At the western end of a long grassy ridge of undulating peaks that sticks into the Hope Valley like a gnarled finger, is 'the shivering mountain' of Mam Tor. Jackdaws and kestrels hang in the wind only yards from the crumbling edge of its grey shale cliff face. It looks as though a giant has sliced off one side of this green hill.

When you peer down through the quivering yellow grass the cars that make their way to the famous Blue John Cavern, marked by a Union Jack bravely fluttering in the strong wind, are mere Dinky toys in the wide sweep of landscape.

Mam Tor - only a jog-trot from the cottages of Castleton - was a popular climbing venue before the last war. In 1931 a woman doctor from Stockport ventured on to its treacherous cliff face and plunged to her death. A few years later two visitors from London were trapped for three hours before rescuers lowered ropes and were able to haul them to safety.

But it is usually on the high moors that people get into serious trouble. It was in appalling weather conditions, on Boxing Day in 1956, that a 21 year old student from Manchester University and his 18 year old girlfriend set out from the Snake Inn to walk to Hayfield.

It would have been a straight-forward hike in the summer months. Now the route along Ashop Clough and over the exposed saddle between Kinder and Mill Hill was covered in snowdrifts. The rushing streams that tumble down from Featherbed Moss were hidden under thick layers of ice. The only shelter available between the Snake Inn and the waterworks buildings at Kinder Reservoir were the ruins of a shooting cabin near Upper Gate Clough. Only part of the stone wall was still standing but it would have provided welcome protection from the chilling wind. The couple passed it by and climbed further up the valley.

For ten hours, search parties with lanterns and whistles ploughed through snow until they found the couple at daybreak, luckily safe and sound. They had huddled together to keep warm and had sung carols all night. An angry policeman said: *"The girl was wearing a blazer, a skirt and two of her father's sweaters. They were a very fortunate couple."*

Another lucky group were three girls and a boy overtaken by darkness on Kinder Scout in February 1964. The boy lit a fire of dead bracken with a cigarette lighter. When it burned out they took it in turns to sit on the warm embers. They had a map and compass but had misread the route, and it was daybreak before a police search party found them.

Michael Parsons, a Manchester boy scout, had an alarming experience in 1957 when mist suddenly swirled around him and eleven other boys as they walked along the west escarpment of Kinder. Michael was heard to cry out in alarm but then he slipped out of sight. The rest of his party stayed together, at first too terrified to move - and their shouts went unanswered.

Many walkers have been caught in similar circumstances. One moment the green waters of the Mermaid Pool 500 feet below are clearly in sight, in another clouds of chilling mist suddenly roll up the rocks and cut visibility to a few yards. *"A dangerous, exhilarating wilderness,"* wrote Rex Bellamy in *The Peak District Companion. "A trackless plateau of peat with no guiding landmarks,"* commented Alfred Wainwright in his *Pennine Way.* Descriptions that these youngsters would now certainly understand

Slowly the party of boys and their Scoutmaster inched their way along the rocks, keeping to high ground and avoiding all declivities in case they too toppled to an unknown fate. It took them six hours to get off the peak and reach a phone box in the valley below. The only clue they could gasp to police and Mountain Rescue men, was the sound of a waterfall they had heard through the mist.

Thirty searchers headed for the Downfall, where the River Kinder falls 500 ft down a series of flat gritstone slabs, and at 5.30am, 12 hours after Michael had vanished, a policeman's torch found the boy wedged against a boulder 50 ft down the rock face. He was carried to Hayfield on a stretcher with head and leg injuries.

Other walkers have been less fortunate than Michael. In 1962 11 year old Mariaka Kluka and her seven-year-old brother Mychalo played truant from school in Glossop and wandered up the Snake Pass road and on to the high heather of Hurst Moor. What happened then will never be known. It was a cold December day. When they were found four days later a box of spent matches showed how they had desperately tried to keep warm before dying of exposure.

But tragedy can also hit well-clad ramblers in the Peak. In 1964 more than 200 Rover Scouts from all over Britain set off in teams of three, at two-minute intervals, on the 50-mile Four Inns Walk around several checkpoints which

# Bodies of two children found on bleak moor following four days' search

THE two Glossop children whose bodies were found on a bleak moor three miles from Glossop died from cold and exposure, it was stated at the inquest at Glossop on Monday. And they came from "a very happy home," their mother stated.

Two other witnesses also expressed the same opinion. The Deputy High Peak Coroner (Mr. H. Hartley) commented: "Here you have two children from a happy home—there is independent evidence of that. Whatever reason caused them to take this journey, it was not unhappiness in the home."

Two Rover Scouts told how they found the bodies huddled together after seeing footprints in the peat. Inspector T. Sanderson said he would like to publicly thank all the people and voluntary organisations who had given assistance to the police in the case, and helped to search. "It was a magnificent response." He mentioned particularly

A sombre headline records the deaths of Mariaka and Mychalo Kluka on the moors above Glossop in December 1962.

Rescuers recover the body of 21 year old Michael Welby from snow covered moors half a mile from the Snake Inn in 1964.

included the famous Cat and Fiddle and Snake Inns, and the Nag's Head at Edale.

Snow covered the moors and a blizzard made conditions very difficult. Some boys took a wrong turning in the mist. Instead of dropping off the moors into Doctor's Gate above Glossop they became disorientated and turned into the Alport valley. Only 33 of the 200 boys finished the walk.

Nineteen year old Gordon Withers collapsed on his way off Bleaklow and died after being rushed to hospital. The following day search teams found the body of 21-year-old John Butterfield in a stream at the head of Alport Dale, and the body of his friend, Michael Welby, was later found, almost covered by snow, about threequarters of a mile away. Both were students at Birmingham University.

The Snake Inn. A favourite starting point for walks over Kinder.

The Four Inns Walk had been well organised with checkpoints every few miles. Little had been left to chance, but the unpredictable Peak District weather had suddenly changed and taken command in a deadly way.

Rescue parties from villages and towns surrounding the Peakland heights never hesitate when emergencies arise, even though the number of false alarms is high. More than once the gale-swept moors have been searched extensively following vague reports of flares or lights seen in the night sky.

Once an airline pilot mistook blazing heather for a crashed plane and started a hunt that went on all night. Two of the rescuers became lost amid the peat bogs of Bleaklow in a severe electrical storm and had to fire Very lights before their comrades could locate them.

Mam Tor, the "shivering mountain". On this slippery shale face a woman doctor fell to her death in 1931.

The Great Ridge can provide a hazardous walk in extreme winter conditions.
This view from Lord's Seat shows Mam Tor on the right, Back Tor on the left.

On another occasion, in the 1930s, Manchester, Sheffield and Chesterfield rambling clubs launched major searches for a young hiker thought to have vanished on Kinder. Eight hundred men joined the hunt. Wives and mothers of the searchers helped the proprietors of Edale's two inns prepare food for the exhausted men, and a sweet manufacturing company distributed free rations of chocolate bars.

For two weeks the search went on, a large bonfire being lit each night as a beacon at the head of Grindsbrook Clough. Then the hiker turned up at Chapel-en-le-Frith - apparently suffering from loss of memory.

One man taking a prominent part in this and other rescue searches, over the years, was Mr John Watson, gamekeeper at Upper House, Kinder, and later a farmer at South Head and The Ashes. He was believed to know Kinder Scout better than anyone in the area and he led many parties over that wild plateau when aircraft came down before and during the war.

Shortly before midnight, on a summer's day in 1937, Mr Harry Porter was going to bed in the Nag's Head Inn at Edale when he heard the sound of aero engines. Somewhere in the clouds above the valley an aircraft appeared to be circling, quite low. Then, through a north-facing window, he saw a sudden blinding flash and heard an explosion. An RAF Heyford bomber of 166 Squadron, on a night-flying exercise from Beverley in Yorkshire, had plunged into the side of Grindslow Knoll. Six young men died. Rescuers from the village brought down their bodies on a rough sledge the following morning.

Another plane was heard circling the rooftops of Glossop on a misty February evening in 1939. No one thought anything about it until the RAF reported that one of their Blenheim bombers was overdue on a night navigational flight from Church Fenton in Yorkshire.

The help of radar and helicopters was not available to search parties in those days and there was no further news of the Blenheim for two weeks. Then Mr Richard Bridge came across scattered wreckage during a ramble across Bleaklow. *"I could not believe my eyes,"* he said later. *"I walked around it for a few minutes."* Then he found two bodies and went for the police.

During the war several more RAF planes were to come to a violent end on the' high moors. And in 1948 13 men of the United States Air Force were killed in a tragic accident only three days before they were due to return to their homes and families across the Atlantic.

Their Superfortress reconnaisance plane was on its way from Scampton, Lincolnshire, to Burtonwood in Lancashire. The cloud base over the Pennines was down to 2,000 ft, and the pilot, Captain Landon P. Tanner, edged nearer to the ground as he made a careful approach to the west. He was on course, though still in cloud, and just coming into radar range of Burtonwood. Then, without warning,

Grindslow Knoll looms over Edale. The village has been the base for many rescue attempts in the Peak hills.

Leaning gate stumps near Dimpus Gate. Swine's Back, on the Kinder plateau, is in the distance.

the plane hit open moorland at the edge of Shelf Moor, two miles from the Snake road, and burst into flames.

At the time two NCOs were finishing an RAF mountain rescue exercise on the Snake Pass. When they picked up a radio message that the plane had crashed they drove to the nearest spot and ran across the moorland towards the flames.

*"We stumbled into holes and jumped over streams,"* said Flight-Sergeant George Thompson, *"But when we climbed on to Shelf Moor we saw it was hopeless. Several bodies were scattered around the wreck."*

For several days the high tail of the aircraft - the only part of the fuselage not devastated by the crash and subsequent fire - could be seen from the Snake road. Even today much of the wreckage remains - the engines, their stainless-steel cowlings still gleaming, and parts of the undercarriage lie half-buried in the black peat just a few feet below the summit of Higher Shelf Stones.

But not all crashes have had such tragic endings. Late one December day in 1945 an RAF Oxford aircraft hit the cloud-covered flank of 1,800 ft high Brown Knoll, near Kinder. On board were two pilots on a refresher flying course after serving in South Africa. With them was their warrant-officer instructor.

Two of the men were trapped in the tangled wreckage. The third man, Flying Officer Ted Croker, was hurled clear. He crawled across to his injured colleagues and wrapped them in parachutes to keep them warm.

Then, despite serious ankle injuries, Croker crawled and tumbled down the hillside. He staggered and rolled through a stream and headed towards a small yellow light gleaming across the valley.

Mr John Shirt of Lee House Farm, Upper Booth, Edale, was having an evening meal when he heard someone calling in the darkness. In the yard outside - where walkers nowadays tramp along the Pennine Way - he found Ted Croker and dragged him into his warm kitchen. All the exhausted bedraggled airman could gasp was *"Plane crash; help my mates."*

Mr Shirt's nephew at once ran down the lane to Upper Booth to phone the police, and Sergeant W.H. Birch of Castleton mustered a squad of experienced gamekeepers, farmers, policemen and RAF personnel to search the moors.

Unable to see their way in the dark the rescuers fell into deep ravines and gulleys and stumbled through hollows filled with ice-cold water. Often the efforts of five or six men were required to drag one of their comrades out of a bog. RAF Very lights arced across the desolate moors between Jacob's Ladder and Colborne.

At dawn RAF planes joined the hunt, though visibility was still bad. Croker had been unable to give any indication of just where the Oxford had come down.

But at 10.30am the cries of Flying Officer J.E. Douthwaite, still huddled in the wreckage, finally led a rescue party to the trapped men.

Two airmen were lucky to escape with their lives when this plane, on an aerial survey, crashed on Kinder Scout in 1963. They spent a night on the exposed moor before RAF mountain rescue men found them.
*Picture by courtesy of the Daily Mail.*

Flying Officer Croker, incidentally, rapidly recovered from his injuries. He later became a well-known secretary of the Football Association.

There was another lucky escape for two civilian airmen, John McWhirter and Dennis Holmes, in 1963 when flying in a twin-engined Rapide aircraft on an aerial survey. They were on their way to Manchester Airport to refuel. *"Everything was normal,"* said Mr McWhirter later, *"But visibility was poor. All of a sudden we appeared to have been caught in a violent down-current. The plane hit the top of Kinder Scout with considerable force and we were both thrown through the nose."*

It was freezing cold and soon it started to rain. The two men sensibly snuggled together in their flying suits to keep warm.

*"We started a search from the Nag's Head at Edale,"* said Pilot Officer Fintan Whyte, leader of an RAF mountain rescue team from Stafford, *"We clambered about the plateau for about four hours. Just 15 minutes of God-sent moonlight enabled me to spot the wreckage. The aircraft was battered beyond belief and it seemed unlikely that anyone could have lived through such a crash. To our amazement a very calm voice from within called out in welcome."*

The lessons from all the accidents on the hills and moors of the Peak are for walkers to take sensible precautions, to wear boots not trainers, to keep a careful check on local weather forecasts. Mountain rescue teams have been much helped nowadays by the widespread use of mobile telephones. Today I seldom venture on to the hills without one. It is a wise precaution.

The rugged paved track over Doctor's Gate that packhorses once trod.

## Chapter Seventeen
# THE ROMAN ROAD

Coldharbour Moor can be a desolate place on a blustery autumn day. It lies on the Pennines just east of the old Derbyshire mill town of Glossop and is one of the highest points at 1,700 feet on the 250 mile Pennine Way, that airy footpath that runs fran Edale to Kirk Yetholm on the Scottish border.

A path from Glossop, which crosses the Pennine Way on Coldharbour Moor, follows one of northern Britain's oldest Roman roads to Hope in the heart of the Peak.

A group of walkers on the Doctor's Gate track across Coldharbour Moor.

It was more than 120 years after Julius Caesar landed on the Channel coast before the Romans extended their empire into northern Britain. Between AD78 and 84 the Governor of Britain, Agricola, ordered several forts to be established in the north of England, linked by military roads.

The Roman surveyors, who always tried to follow high land and avoid the swampy undrained valleys, connected their newly built fort at Glossop to a remote fortified station near Hope, called Navio, which lay on an important hilltop road running from Sheffield to Buxton.

Much of the route from Glossop can still be followed and from Melandra Castle, on the outskirts of Glossop, this excellent walk along the Roman road can be started.

The Roman road that climbs along the shoulder of Win Hill to Hope Woodlands.

Little remains of Melandra today. The foundations of its walls form a large square, about 120 yards wide, on an open grassy promontory above the River Etherow, where pensioners now exercise their dogs and children race up and down the sandy slopes on BMX bikes.

Over the centuries the stonework was plundered for nearby buildings. Most of it is thought to be within half a mile of the castle. During the last war, the Glossop Home Guard did not help, either, when they dug trenches across the site and mounted machine-gun posts in case German paratroops decided to land nearby.

Beyond the quiet streets of Old Glossop, a path alongside the stream brings one to a sheep farm at Mossylee, where the path starts to climb along Doctor's Gate - the gateway to the high moors. On the right can be seen a small artificial lake where Lord Howard's gamekeepers once reared 1,000 wild duck each year for the pleasure of the shooting fraternity - they also raised 2,000 pheasants lower down the valley.

The track to Hope turns up a gully at the head of the valley along a route that has been known as Doctor's Gate for 350 years. "Gate" is the old Derbyshire word for road or track and the "doctor" is thought to have been a 15th century Vicar of Glossop, Dr John Talbot, son of the Earl of Shrewsbury, who presumably travelled to his father's castle in Sheffield along this route in pre-turnpike days.

This is the best preserved length of the Roman road to Hope. Slabs of gritstone have been set on edge, about a yard wide at the most, with 'kerbstones' at either side. Heather and bilberry have covered some of the track but the paved length can be followed for several hundred yards. Regrettably, although this may well be a former Roman road, the stones as we see them laid today do not conform to what scholars inform us was normal Roman practice. A traveller writing about the Peak District 90 years ago, described the road as being five feet wide, which is nearer the width of traditional Roman roads. Was this road narrowed earlier in the century and records of the work lost?

From here the old route continues along the A57 Glossop-to-Sheffield road which winds down the spectacular Snake Valley.

The river is crossed by a plain footbridge and a track climbs to Hope Cross, with the long, thin western arm of Ladybower Reservoir curving into the hazy distance. On the summit of the ridge there are views that are hard to match anywhere in Peakland. To the north the Woodlands Valley skirts the steeply-sloped meadows of Rowlee Pasture, and the eye can follow the course of Alport Dale as far as a green plantation of conifers cloaking its western wall across from Alport Castles - a turretted outcrop of splintered rock that is the nearest Derbyshire can offer to the spectacular stone pinnacles of Arizona. Beyond lies the flattened brown mound of Bleaklow, the wildest and most remote area of the High Peak.

The Roman road to Hope slips over the Hope Woodlands ridge at its slenderest point and follows a hollow way down the western side of Hope Brink. Dense bracken is on either side. The village of Hope lies ahead. Behind the church a small stone bridge spans a sluggish stream that runs into the Noe. It was here that the Romans probably made a ford to reach their fort to the east.

A field path leads to the site of Navio in a sea of cattle-filled meadows and a triangle of lanes. It is sited on a high flat meadow above the stream with just one or two slabs of stone marking the site of the ancient military post. No other remains are to be seen, despite considerable excavations some years ago. Nevertheless, a splendid Roman altar, now resting in Weston Park Museum, Sheffield, was discovered as recently as 1980 by a farmer ploughing nearby. Perhaps more remnants will eventually come to light.

St Peter's Church, Hope, which dates from the 13th Century. A headless 9th Century preaching cross stands in the graveyard.

The ancient track dropping down the bracken-covered slopes of Hope Brink. In the distance lies Crookstone Knoll, the eastern end of the Kinder plateau.

All that now remains of the ancient Roman station of Navio between Hope and Bradwell.

## Chapter Eighteen
# BILL AT THE CROWN

The inns of the Peak have been welcome refuges for walkers for centuries, and many are the stories told about the old stone-walled ale houses in the days before they became the comfortable food and drink establishments so familiar to us today.

It is claimed, for example, that in 1804 the first Bakewell pudding was made by mistake at the Rutland Arms in the town - an egg mixture meant for the pastry of a jam tart being accidentally poured into the jam.

Highwayman Dick Turpin is said to have called at the Bull's Head in Little Hucklow, Hayfield's Royal Hotel was once a vicarage, the Izaac Walton in Dovedale was a 17th Century farmhouse, Byron and Ruskin are thought to have stayed at the New Bath in Matlock, a well inside the bar of the Red Lion at Birchover was once in frequent use, and gangs of Irish navvies fought on the sand-covered taproom floor of the Cross Keys in Chapel Milton when George Wilks was the landlord in 1910.

The landlords of these inns were often quite extraordinary characters. In more recent times I recall the licensee of the Pack Horse near New Mills calling on his customers to leave the bar and help him round up several of his pigs that had escaped from a paddock and were now galloping down the road. Some people in

The Royal Hotel at Hayfield. Since it was built in 1755 it has served as a parsonage, a pub (the Shoulder of Mutton), a vicarage and an hotel.

Mottram, near Glossop, may remember the bearded landlord of a well-known inn who occasionally walked into the bar with an air rifle and took pot shots at balloons tethered to the ceiling.

There were many others. I have vivid memories of big Bill Berrisford who had a voice like a trombone together with a booming laugh that shook the rafters of the former Crown Inn at Dove Holes in the 1940s. He had only one good leg, but he stumped around the bar each morning, as agile as Long John Silver, pouring sawdust from a sack, into a row of cast iron spittoons under the plain wooden benches of the tap room, then mopping the tiled floor before throwing buckets' full of water and bars of red carbolic soap into the drain of the open air urinal across the inn yard.

Bill was 17 when he lost his leg. He was working in a Peak District quarry during one of the many controlled explosions that brought cliff sides of brown and white limestone tumbling to the valley floor. A tiny, marble- sized piece of rock struck him on the shin one winter's day in 1923 and crippled him for life.

During the 1930s he helped his father run the Crown in Dove Holes, which was at that time a nondescript collection of grey stone houses covered in lime dust, with six shops, four pubs, a church, a chapel and a cricket ground. Across the road from the Crown, in the shadow of a miniature Alpine landscape of mottled grey slag heaps of waste lime known as 'ess hills', lay the Bull Ring, a circular mound of closely cropped grass that was formerly an ancient henge monument of stone slabs. All of the slabs had been carted away by local farmers over the years.

The Crown was the quarrymen's favourite inn. When they finished their shift, they would stamp through the front door wearing hobnailed boots and 'yorks' - leather-belted moleskin or corduroy trousers tied with string or a strap just below the knee. They were usually covered in a thin patina of white dust that deposited itself in a trail along the passage as they made towards the bar.

The bar was little more than a short side counter with a glass partition above it. There were no pump handles. Instead, beer was poured into glasses from a tall white jug that Bill had to refill from wooden barrels in the cellar below.

Some of the quarrymen who frequented the inn worked long after normal retirement age. A good example was old George Naden, a stone filler with piercing blue eyes and a frothy white beard, who was born in 1857 and was still working at the age of 74. Others included Jim Lomas who acquired a reputation as the Dove Holes quarries' strong man. *"He's the best man I know with a No. 10 shovel,"* said Bill. And there was Tom Fletcher, a cheery shunter employed in nearby Small Dale.

This group played dominoes on the taproom table along with old, whiskery Herbert Jennings, a Boer War veteran whose raucous coughing sometimes stopped play for lengthy periods.

A flight of damp wooden steps led into the cellar where a fresh barrel would be uncorked with blows from a stout hammer that hung on the whitewashed wall, and the dark frothy beer was poured into Bill's white jug. The Crown was an ale house, licensed only for the sale of beer. Bottles of lemonade and packets of crisps could also be purchased, and Players cigarettes.

Nevertheless, a few dark bottles were kept on the top shelf of a cupboard in the living room. Whenever the local police sergeant called at the inn - by the rear door, of course - some of the contents of one of the bottles was poured into a small glass and given to the officer as he stood in a dark corner of the passage without his helmet, rocking gently on his heels.

There was a lot of shouting in the tap room most evenings and sometimes, despite his one leg, Bill could be seen helping a retching man out through the back door. On summer weekends a crowd of cricketers swarmed into the inn from the field across the road. There was even more shouting and carousing if the Dove Holes team had beaten the nearby village of Chapel-en-le-Frith, their arch-rivals in the High Peak League.

The Crown had a special front parlour known as the Ladies' Room. This was occupied only on Sunday evenings when a few couples sat on leather-topped bench seats at iron clawfoot tables and listened to popular music played on an ancient upright piano in one corner. Occasionally, the pianist was accompanied by a wild-eyed local wag who, fortified with a few pints of Bell's Best Bitter, would

use a couple of kitchen knives and an upturned biscuit tin as a kettle drum. *"He's very good, he should be in a band,"* someone once said. *"Yes, a Band of Hope,"* commented Bill with a guffaw.

The Buff Room was at the top of the stairs. The local branch of the Royal Antedeluvian Order of Buffaloes, a friendly society sometimes unkindly referred to as the *"poor man's Masons"*, met here once a month, and the door had a sliding panel that enabled members' identities to be established before they entered.

Needless to say, when an adult was needed to don a red robe and white whiskers for Christmas Day dinner, his sisters and performing troupe of young nephews always clamoured for Uncle Bill. Although he had spent many gruelling hours on his peg-leg, with his noisy customers on the previous night, he still made a marvellous Father Christmas.

Bill Berrisford, landlord of the former Crown Inn at Dove Holes.

One of the locomotives that hauled Paddy's Mail crosses Church Street, Hayfield,
on its way from the station to the reservoir site in 1903.

Bowden Bridge which carried packhorses over the River Kinder.
The reservoir railway ran along the river bank just beyond the stone arch.

# Chapter Nineteen
## PADDY'S MAIL

Everything stopped when "Paddy's Mail" steamed across the cobbles of Church Street in Hayfield a century ago. Little girls in neat white pinafores, and small boys in stiff collars, knee breeches and laced-up boots, gathered in droves as a fussy steam engine and four red carriages packed with grinning workmen skirted the side wall of the George Inn and rumbled past the windows of Lathams' store.

This was a daily spectacle in the little village in the first decade of the last century. Most walkers who amble through Hayfield today are completely unaware of the Kinder Railway that crossed two streets and ran up the valley for a couple of miles.

It was all due to the building of Kinder Reservoir. The track, which ran from Hayfield Station to the dam site, was laid down in 1903 by contractors working for Stockport Corporation. Trains transported equipment and materials as well as ferrying the many Irish navvies employed on the job, up to the head of the valley.

Abram Kellett, a stocky, bowler-hatted civil-engineer who was in charge of the project, ran the trains up a ramp from the station (now a car park), across Station Road and through a gap alongside the old George Inn - where a cottage had to be demolished - to reach the main village thoroughfare, Church Street. This, of course, was 70 years before the present A 624 bypass was built behind the George.

The single-track line then dropped down a short alleyway alongside the village store, crossed the River Kinder on a trestle bridge near the present Royal Hotel car park and traversed a wide curve over the cricket field. Excavated earth, removed to make way for the track and heaped against the northern wall,

A farm track that traverses the Kinder valley today. South Head and Mount Famine are in the distance.

provides spectators at Hayfield Cricket Club with a grandstand view of play to this day.

The route of the line then crossed a recreation ground before hugging the banks of the River Kinder through a tree-crammed gorge to the flat meadow which is now a National Park camping site. At Bowden Bridge, a simple stone arched structure on an old packhorse route, the rails crossed the River Sett near its junction with the Kinder stream and went up the fields below Hill Houses to Booth Bridge. From here to the dam itself, the line followed the route of the private waterworks road that now runs to a filter house standing below a great grass covered earth embankment holding back 500 million gallons of drinking water.

The sound of a piercing whistle and a plume of white smoke from the tall chimney of a stubby engine became a common sight in Hayfield village, and along the valley. Eight hundred men were employed on the reservoir project. Many had lodgings in New Mills; others lived in large barrack-style huts above Booth Bridge and lower down the valley near Oak Bank.

Hayfield Parish Council received complaints about the excessive speed of trains steaming along the valley. *"Drivers get up speed when leaving the cricket field and rush along at a quick rate, over the crossing at Watery Hey Bridge,"* wrote a local commentator in a newspaper.

In 1904 there was further anxiety when an outbreak-of smallpox occurred among workmen employed at the dam site.

In one of the huts near Bowden Bridge lived Mr and Mrs Dove, engaged by the contractors to provide bed, breakfast and evening meal for the navvies. To cater for the hungry men the Doves had sacks of potatoes and flour piled high in a store room. Home-cured bacon hung from hooks on the beams, eggs were obtained from dozens of hencotes lining the river bank and goats grazed in the field.

The huts had been built as far as possible out of sight of the grouse moors over Kinder Scout, the 2,000-ft high hill owned by the wealthy Manchester textile baron, Mr James Watts, who also had a summer home at Farlands near Booth Bridge. The sight of this untidy camp and its bustling population of navvies upset him so much that he moved to Upper House, a remote farm high up the valley above the dam's water line. He renovated the property and planted a large wood of conifers to screen the reservoir from his windows.

There were many visitors at Upper House, particularly during the shooting season. Mrs Humphry Ward, the Victorian novelist, wrote part of her *History of David Grieve* while staying there. Agatha Christie spent several weekends as a guest.

By 1912 the great earth embankment, nearly 1,200 feet long and 116 feet high, was complete, and water was lapping against the top stones. The navvies departed, much of the Kinder Railway track was lifted, and only two locomotives were left. The line from Hayfield Station to Cuckoo's Nest Quarry was kept open until 1915, then that too was removed, and the Kinder Railway was no more.Its route, however, can still be followed, though the fields through which it passed are private.

Of course, even the most elderly of today's villagers were born too late to see "Paddy's Mail" steaming through the trees and rattling over the loose cobbles of Church Street. But it has never been forgotten - it must have been quite a sight.

Paddy's Mail steams along the lane towards the present-day gates of Kinder Reservoir with the river at its side.
*Historical pictures by courtesy of New Mills Local History Society.*

Kinder Reservoir.  Today it holds 500 million gallons of water.

Crag Hall, the Earl of Derby's occasional shooting lodge, with Shutlingsloe beyond.

The Crag Inn on the banks of the Clough Brook.
In the 17th Century it was known as Bottom o'th' Bank Farm.

## Chapter Twenty
# RIVERSIDE TRAILS

The River Kinder is little more than a short but charming mountain stream, although, when strong west winds blow, clouds of spray plume upwards spectacularly where the water falls over the Downfall. The Peak District, however, possesses many other beautiful rivers that offer a variety of walks along their shelving banks.

A stroll along the banks of the upper River Dane is not easy to find because much of the stream is almost buried beneath a sea of tangled bracken in a steep-sided, and privately-owned, valley. My old friend, Douglas Young, who has walked these hills for many years, has frequently splashed through the Dane's numerous small waterfalls, clambering over moss-covered boulders. When I once accompanied him on an unsuccessful fishing trip, I had to agree that it was "tiger country" that left me quite out of breath.

So it is wiser to turn to the Dane's Clough Brook tributary which traverses Wildboarclough, surely one of the least-spoiled parts of the Peak and one easily accessible by road. The stream first sees the light of day on the heathery south face of Shining Tor, but the valley through which it then tumbles is best approached from Macclesfield Forest.

The whole vale is laid out at one's feet from the saddle at Big Stone. The mass of Whetstone Ridge lies to the east, fold after fold like so many rolls of brown carpet, and the tiny buildings of the Cat and Fiddle Inn are just visible in haze at the head of Goyts Clough.

To the north lies Shining Tor, its higher slopes touched with powder-blue mist in mid-morning, and the main road between Macclesfield and Buxton winding around the contours below its airy summit. In a hollow below the road lies Field Head farm, and it was here on a dreadful day in May 1989 that the full effects of a colossal downpour on the hill above were felt by farmer Edward Nixon and his family.

*"I was indoors having a cup of tea"' Mr Nixon told me. "The storm suddenly broke and it seemed to be right over our farm. Water about two feet deep swirled around the buildings and even came up the waste pipe and filled our bath. I had lived at Field House for 25 years and I had never seen anything like this. The water even came through the back wall."*

Five cows were swept down the Clough Brook. One came ashore comparatively unhurt but dazed at Clough House Farm, but was then swept a further two miles downstream. Near the farm a road bridge and a weir were tossed away in the torrent. Cages of rocks, each weighing three tons and used to stabilise the banks, were carried off in a 'tidal wave' that demolished thousands of yards of stone walls and caused damage estimated at £1,000,000.

Mrs Sheila Bowler and her husband John were returning from Leek Market to Torgate Farm, at the head of the valley, when the storm started. Their prized Gritstone sheep had just finished lambing and several were washed away. *"It was the most frightening day of my life."* she said.

Luckily, according to the National Rivers Authority, the kind of freak storm that fell on Shining Tor that day and swept through Wildboarclough with such devastation, is likely to occur only once in 500 years.

Swallows swoop around the buildings of Clough House Farm in summer. On the steep slopes of the surrounding hills scores of sheep graze, many of them speckle-faced mules - Swaledales crossed with Blue-faced Leicesters. The shadows of clouds run along the rumpled folds of Shutlingsloe, leaping over the valleys and darting up the slopes without a check.

Clough House Farm dates back to the 17th Century and the car park which lies at the side of Clough Brook, sheltered by willows and rowan trees, attracts motorists and walkers starting out down the valley. The farmer, Mr John Eardley, is renowned both for his prize-winning sheep and for his conservation work. In 1997 he won first prize in the Cheshire Farms Competition for the best sheep flock and in the following year the award for the best farm buildings.

Mr Eardley says that conservation farming is his only interest. *"When I started putting up dry stone walls I was told there was no way farming would ever pay for them. I think I've proved that wrong,"* he says.

Walkers find Mr Eardley helpful and friendly. He welcomes visitors to the valley with a bright twinkle in his eye. I have watched him, clad in his long rubber waders, dipping sheep on the banks of the brook, and on another occasion layering thorn hedges at the side of the lane. *"We must make the place look neat and tidy,"* he said.

The dramatic view as one approaches Wildboarclough from the Cat and Fiddle road.

The full splendour of Shutlingsloe (1,659 feet) can best be appreciated from Crag Hall or the lane nearby.

There are three routes down Wildboarclough from Clough House. A high stile on the right of the lane leads to a narrow footpath through a sea of bracken and across the shoulder of 1,659-ft high Shutlingsloe, with the stream out of sight below dense woodland. But this path can be soggy in wet weather. A middle route follows the lane which accompanies the winding stream and gives excellent views of its little peat-stained pools and splashing waterfalls, and often glimpses of a heron that alights on the banks and dippers that flit from boulder to boulder.

But my favourite route is along a high lane that leads past Crag Hall, a shooting lodge used by the Earl of Derby but now converted into apartments. In December, shooting parties turn up at the hall and sit shivering in the woods while beaters move down from the moor above.

Brian Worsley, who lived at the hall for many years, assured me that most pheasants seemed to escape. As we chatted outside his cottage on a very cold day, the encircling hills covered with white and snow flurries creating patterns of broken white lace on the nearby walls, the valley echoed with the crackle of gunfire. Land Rovers filled the yard of the hall waiting for their owners to return. One lucky pheasant zoomed over our heads away from the firing line and escaped down the valley. *"I like to see that,"* said Brian.

Crag Hall was originally built as a private home around 1800 by a Staffordshire man who established a calico printing factory in the vale below. It then became one of the Earl of Derby's shooting lodges at the end of the 19th Century. The view from the elegant building's terraced garden looks down a meadow and across the stream to the 'miniature Matterhorn' of Shutlingsloe which dominates the valley. The tiny pink buildings of Banktop and Higher Bank are seen perched high on its shoulder.

Clough Brook hugs the lane that runs through Wildboarclough.

St Saviour's Church, Wildboarclough.
Few churches in Britain can equal the tranquillity of this site in a wooded ravine.

On a late autumn day in 1996 I arrived to find the meadow a hive of activity. A large marquee had been erected, its sides flapping in the breeze, and there was a dry smell of fallen leaves. The air was full of whistles.

The BBC were filming one of their *One Man and his Dog* TV programmes and groups of sheep, provided by Mr Ben Kidd of Holt Farm just over the hill, were being steered through sets of white gates by a succession of border collies. A number of spectators, well wrapped-up in anoraks, their feet covered in blankets, sat on chairs below the wall of the hall garden, and one cameraman lurked behind a bush planted at the side of the field. Another cameraman huddled precariously at the top of a mass of scaffolding. A maze of cables linked the scene to several vans in the hall yard.

At the foot of a dell, crowded with rhododendrons, lies St Saviour's Church, built by the Earl of Derby around 1901 as a memorial for the safe return of his five sons from the Boer War. The stone building, with its squat crenellated tower, stands amid a lawn and graveyard that is immaculately maintained. Tall Scots pines lean over the nave windows and rhododendron bushes brush the pink walls. It is little wonder that Granada TV shot several scenes here for their *Jewel in the Crown* serial - St Oswald's was a realistic substitute for a church in the Himalayas.

Below the church the Clough Brook surges under Crag Bridge where the remains of two large old mills can still be found under the trees and shrubs. The only substantial part remaining is a wing of the Upper Works which is now a private house and was at one time Wildboarclough's village post office. Brian Worsley remembers that the top floor of this three-storey building was used as a tenants' leisure room. *"We had a billiards table in it"*, he says. *"And during the war, when it was a Government store, Dutch soldiers stood guard there all day."*

On the far bank of the stream stands the picturesque Crag Inn. Inside there is a cosy bar with a welter of black beams. When I gossiped with landlord John Burgess many years ago no thought of exploiting the natural water of Wildboarclough seemed to have entered his head. But when he left the inn in the 1970s, to live in Old Beams Cottage nearby, he obtained permission to drill 125 feet down through the valley's gritstone and eventually discovered a large underground reservoir of pure water.

Now Wildboarclough Water is on sale in shops throughout the country. Each week a 2,000-gallon stainless steel tanker pumps water from the well behind the cottage and takes it to a bottling plant at Leek, 15 miles away. John invested his life savings into the project and it has proved to be a winner.

Walkers proceeding down the valley lane are accompanied by the rush and gurgle of the trout-dimpled brook at their side and it is only when the stream hurries under the Buxton to Congleton road at Allgreave that it vanishes in a steep-sided, privately-owned gorge. It meets the River Dane just above Danebridge at the foot of a steep hill from the hamlet of Wincle and from here further riverside paths can be followed on to the Cheshire Plain and back towards Gradbach.

It is always with a profound sense of regret that I turn my back on the Clough Brook. I find it soothing and companionable as I walk along the lane with the scented darkness of the bordering pines, the stone walls spotted with crusty brown and yellow lichens and the nearby pastures dappled with the year's first bleating lambs.

After rising on Axe Edge the River Wye flows through Buxton's Pavilion Gardens before plunging underground.

The Clough Brook flows through gritstone country and the scenery is quite different from that found in areas where limestone is the dominant rock. The engaging River Wye, which graces Buxton's Pavilion Gardens before plunging into a culvert under the town's Crescent and shopping streets, rises amid gritstone boulders on the slopes of Axe Edge but eventually runs gaily through Ashwood Dale - in the heart of the limestone Peak.

The rocky footpath from the bottom of Taddington Dale along the banks of the Wye hugs a dense scree of woodland and follows a great curve around the craggy escarpment of 1,000-ft high Fin Cop. The trees echo to the piping of chaffinches and great tits, and where the river widens below the arches of Monsal Dale viaduct, trout splash the surface faster than a boy can pitch pebbles into the slow moving water.

If one climbs up to the Monsal Head Hotel, with its plain chairs, blazing coal fire and cheerful landlord, the view up the vale is little different from that described by Edward Bradbury more than a 100 years ago. *"Blue smoke from a farm house curls up the grassy slopes like incense, the stream ripples between the knees of cattle standing in the cool water."*

It is the old disused railway viaduct, built in 1860, that dominates the scene, however. A walkers' path, the Monsal Trail, crosses the structure which is designated a *"building of historical and architectural interest."*

The path crosses a thistle-filled field to a stone and steel footbridge where I once met a group of ramblers in bright red and blue anoraks perched on the iron railings. In Bradbury's day this was a rustic wooden plank bridge resting on rough piles of stones *"to delight the soul of a painter."* It is still in a charming setting today, with a farmhouse nearby and goats grazing amid apple trees.

A lane climbs up the valley with the Wye murmuring on the left. At Upperdale, where a small road bridge crosses the river to give access to the tiny station of Monsal Dale that once stood on piles on the far hillside, I once met the genial water bailiff for the Chatsworth Estate. *"I've got two anglers coming from Lincolnshire today,"* he told me. *"But the water's a bit cloudy after last night's rain and they may find the fishing a bit poor until later in the afternoon. I'll let them return another day without charge."* As we talked, sunlight caught the hilltops near Litton, higher up the valley, and sent a bright, warming light over the crags on Hay Top.

A few years ago Cressbrook Mill was in ruins, the hands of its big clock caked in rust. In the last century, when Bradbury walked past, old people living at Cressbrook still remembered the days when child workers walked three miles to church in Tideswell. There was abundant water to drive two large waterwheels, which have now vanished, but water still boils over a weir next to the mill, a haze of spray often being thrown back by a strong breeze.

*"Between Litton Mills and Cressbrook, one of the least known and loveliest portions of the river runs between limestone cliffs and steep wood-covered hills,"* wrote Bradbury. *"There is no river path here. The Wye is locked in by sheer precipices."*

Nowadays a carefully preserved path hugs the river side under the frowning grey cliffs. This is the gorge of Water-cum-Jolly. Great buttresses of rock squeeze the milky-coloured water into a narrow, high-walled passage and the path twists along the north bank past patches of wild rhubarb and cow parsley.

Bradbury left the Wye at Litton Mill, a nondescript huddle of buildings, and went on to Eyam. Now there is a handy youth hostel with 76 beds, showers and a games room at nearby Ravenstor but I usually turn towards the George at Tideswell. After all, I have often thought, if the hard-worked children employed at Cressbrook Mill could walk the three miles to the village, so can I.

The footbridge that crosses the Wye below Monsal Head.

The preserved railway viaduct in Monsal Dale that is now in use as a walkers' footpath.
Here the river bends around the wooded slope of Fin Cop.

The medieval bridge at Bakewell. One of the most attractive town views in the Peak.

Access to Haddon Hall is gained over the Wye by this handsome stone-arched bridge.

A sheer limestone cliff at Water-cum-Jolly near Cressbrook Mill, at the side of the Wye, attracts rock climbers each weekend.

The lower reaches of the River Wye should never be ignored either. One enjoyable stroll is from Rowsley, where the river slips unobtrusively into the Derwent under a fine multi-arched bridge, to the pleasing town of Bakewell. On the bank stands Caudwell's Mill, a large three-storeyed structure of silver-grey stone which continues to produce flour by water power. A stile leads to the banks of the Wye and on to Dove House Farm, with the river glinting through trees as it corkscrews across flat green meadows.

There are no public footpaths alongside the Wye until Haddon Hall but a narrow stone-walled lane leads to the main A6 road. A short walk along the road, with the woods of Haddon on the right, precedes another stile and a path through the trees. Then a footbridge in the woods gives access to a pleasant mossy path on the north bank of the river.

Through the trees are glimpsed the turrets and battlements of Haddon Hall, one of the finest medieval manor houses in the country. Its paved courtyard, long gallery and chapel, which dates from Norman times, are joys to behold, but its greatest popular appeal is perhaps the story of Dorothy Vernon, daughter of the squire of Haddon, who was supposed to have eloped across the Wye with her lover John Manners in the 16th Century. The legend first appeared in print in 1820 and has since been the subject of several romantic novels and at least one film.

In fact, movie makers have often been drawn to Haddon. Its fine courtyard and battlements can be seen in *The Lady and the Highwayman, Elizabeth, The Princess Bride, The Prince and the Pauper, Lady Jane* and particularly in the latest Franco Zeffirelli version of *Jane Eyre.*

The river flows in serpentine loops through meadows bordering the A6. Alders and willow bang over the banks and Friesian cattle flick their tails in the shallows. A clearly-marked path wanders under a frieze of trees and hugs the bank all the way to Bakewell with its handsome church, bustling market and noisy mallards flocking around the weir.

I have sat quietly by the side of the Wye in the Haddon meadow on many occasions, the river sparkling in summer sun, ruffled by the winter winds. In summer marsh marigolds shine like orchids in the wet meadow grass, the sun pours dusty gleams of light through the leaves of the trees and a smell of sun-baked grass and herbs wafts by on the breeze.

The silvery Wye winds through the alders and beech trees that line
its banks between Haddon and Bakewell.

The Swiss Lake above Chatsworth House. It provides water for the famous Cascade and the great fountain in the gardens below.

The historic pile of Carl Wark lies amid wild moorland between Burbage and Millstone Edges.

## Chapter Twenty-one
# THE ROCKY RIM

It is only a few miles from the fertile valley of the Wye, and its flower-speckled bankside meadows, to the Peak District's rocky eastern rim. For more than 20 miles a splintered, jagged escarpment runs high above the River Derwent. Great sweeps of moorland stretch away towards the distant rooftops of Sheffield and Chesterfield - and lucky are the hillwalkers who live in or near these towns, only a short distance from some of the most majestic countryside in England.

Beeley is a sleepy little hamlet with many pretty cottages, some covered in roses. A climb up to Beeley Plantation can be exhausting until a wide track crossing Beeley Moor is reached. Ahead lie the woods that provide a dramatic back-drop to Chatsworth House.

The hall itself, which stands close to the Derwent, was not visible as I walked along an estate road of fine limestone chippings one spring day. Tall, smooth trunks of sitka spruce and lodgepole pine lined the road, and the wind whistled through their spiky branches. Lambs were bleating loudly in a sheltered field just below Bunker's Hill Wood.

Then a sheet of silver glinted through the trees and 1 reached the bank of Swiss Lake. An empty house stood among trees on the far side. Coot and Canada geese were on the water and the short grass at my feet was bright with bugle, buttercup, campion and speedwell.

Swiss Lake, and Emperor Lake nearby, were laid out by the fourth Duke of Devonshire more than 200 years ago to provide water for Chatsworth House, its various outbuildings, the famous Cascade and its giant fountain. Few visitors venture beyond Chatsworth's gardens, and these stretches of open water in their sylvan setting amid the estate's 1,900 acres of woodland, remain comparatively undisturbed.

Within a few minutes I came to the Hunting Tower - a slight divergence from my route but one well worth making - which stands on a prominent headland overlooking Chatsworth Park. This slender 90 ft high Elizabethan building is said to have been erected to give the Duchess and her lady guests a wide bird's eye view of the park when foxes, hares or deer were being hunted. But modern day experts have described it as *"the oldest free standing purpose-built folly in Britain."*

The tower has four bell-shaped cupolas and many latticed windows - and also a TV aerial on the roof! Three iron Crimea cannons, the wheels of their wooden carriages sunk in concrete amid the bracken, overlook the park. They were last fired when Queen Victoria visited Chatsworth.

The church at Edensor. In the foreground are the Cavendish graves and a memorial stone laid by President Kennedy in 1963.

Across the valley I could see the rooftops of Edensor village and its tall church steeple. The tree-covered mound of Calton Pastures lay like a huge upturned boat in front of the great house.

A squelchy path dropped down to the Chesterfield road just above the Robin Hood Inn and from there was a path up the grey crags of Birchen Edge and on to a heather-covered moor.

Perched on a large gritstone boulder on the 1,000-ft contour is the Nelson Monument, a thin miniature Cleopatra's Needle, about eight feet high. It was erected by John Brightman, a patriotic Baslow man, in 1810, only five years after the Battle of Trafalgar. Oddly enough, the date 1905 has been carved on the monument's eastern face for some mysterious reason.

Rugged Gardom's Edge overlooks the Bar Brook valley, a pleasant landscape of green meadows and copses of oak and sycamore. Beyond the Sheffield road, another monument, equally as grotesque as the Nelson pillar, perches at the end of Baslow Edge. This ten foot high stone cross is in memory of the Duke of Wellington and was erected in 1866.

Much more appealing are the natural rock formations that occur along all the west-facing edges of Derbyshire. Kinder Scout and Derwent Edge have many and on this day I came across other boulders that had been serrated, smoothed and sculpted by the winds and rain of centuries.

Not far from Wellington's Monument is the Eagle Stone, an impressive chunk of gritstone standing in splendid isolation on the moor. The western face is weathered into several smooth grooves and must be quite difficult to climb - but climbers frequently do.

The meadows of Hassop and Pilsley spread away for several miles, the grassy rectangles fusing mistily into copses of trees as the slope runs away to the hidden River Wye near Bakewell and the old sheepwash bridge at Ashford-in-the-Water.

The Eagle Stone on Baslow Edge. One of the most distinctive weathered rock formations in the Peak.

The gorge of Middleton Dale, rimmed with high limestone cliffs, runs to the north-west and the houses of Curbar - *"a grey little village with a stranded look"* - are only a mile below the rocks of the escarpment.

There is a good, smooth, sandy track along Baslow Edge, although I found it considerably chewed up in places by horses' hooves, and it was not long before I crossed a gap where the old road to Bleak House and Chesterfield pinches through the rocks, and headed north along Curbar Edge.

Several climbers were resting at the foot of Great Buttress, a prominent nose of gritstone. Grey-naped jackdaws hovered around the jumble of crags. Curlews and skylarks were circling high over the moor on my right and the dark heather was sprinkled with small white flowers.

Below lay the River Derwent, much nearer now, with the lovely arched bridge at Calver clearly in view. Close by stood Calver Mill, a severe building with two end towers and many storeys of windows - little wonder it stood in as Colditz Castle for a TV drama series.

The track along Froggatt Edge, which is the northern continuation of Curbar Edge, was wide and sandy. Dense bracken and silver birch were on either side as I dropped down from a sea of heather that stretched across the moor to the crest of White Edge. The upper valley of the Derwent opened before me with Mam Tor at its head and silver railway lines emerging from Dore and Totley Tunnel just beneath my feet at Grindleford.

At the Fox House Inn, where guests overflowing from the Duke of Rutland's grouse-shooting lodge at nearby Longshaw sometimes slept on the floor, I crossed the A625 and headed up a flinty path to Carl Wark, an ancient fortress perched on

A craggy outcrop of gritstone rocks near Curbar Gap. The old road to Chesterfield pierces the Peak District's "rocky rim" at this point and there is a car park for walkers.

Flat rocks rim Curbar Edge. The escarpments of Baslow and Fallinge Edges lie beyond.

a small plateau, defended on three sides by precipitous walls and on the fourth by a ten foot high rampart of boulders backed by turf. When was it built and why? Despite a certain amount of excavation no one seems to know.

Less than half a mile farther on stands Higger Tor, at 1,418 ft overlooking both Carl Wark and the valley. Conifers now cover much of the banks of the stream that rushes down from Hallam Moor, and beyond lie the vertical slabs of Burbage Edge.

It was a short stroll down a lane and through fields to Hathersage to end one of my many lovely walks along the rim of the Peak. And it is fitting that the large village of Hathersage with its hillside homes, noble church and historic old vicarage should be the last place to visit in this book.

From the windows of the vicarage, Charlotte Bronte, as explained in Chapter 3, looked across the crowded graveyard, with its leaning algae-covered tombstones, to the green tree-dappled valley below the church. Cattle grazed, as they still do, on the banks of the tumbling Hood Brook and the dark crags of Stanage Edge etched the skyline beyond. It is a view that still encapsulates the magic and grandeur of the Peak District today.

## SOME CHURNET VALLEY TITLES STILL AVAILABLE

**THE ASHBOURNE CIRCLE**   John and Ann Gilman        ISBN 1897949 94 4        £ 8.95

**HISTORY OF DEVONSHIRE ROYAL HOSPITAL**   M. Langham & C. Wells        £ 9.95

**DOWN THE COBBLED STONES**   John Lea        ISBN 1 897949 45 6        £ 7.95

**HAPPY HIGHWAYS**: The Highlands of Staffordshire Revisited  Ray Poole        £ 6.95

**HIGHLANDS OF STAFFORDSHIRE**   W.H.Nithsdale 1906 (facsimile)        £ 6.95

**LAND OF THE DOVE**   David J. Ford        ISBN 1 897949 56 1        £ 8.95

**LAND OF THE ETHEROW**   Neville T. Sharpe        ISBN 1897949 68 5        £ 9.95

**MACCLESFIELD AT WAR**   Philip McGuinness        ISBN 1 897949 84 7        £ 9.95

**MEMORIES OF GLOSSOPDALE**   Mollie Carney        ISBN 1 897949 89 8        £ 9.95

**THE PEAK DISTRICT AT WAR**   Peter Clowes        ISBN 1897949 76 6        £ 7.95

**PEAKLAND PICKINGS**   Neville T. Sharpe        ISBN 1 897949 51 0        £ 7.95

**WHEN I WAS A CHILD**   Shaw 1904 (facsimile) Illustrated ISBN 1 897949 46 4        £12.95

**RUDYARD REFLECTIONS**   Basil Jeuda        ISBN 1897949 74 X        £ 7.95

**STAFFORDSHIRE REGIMENTS** 1705-1919  Vols I and II  Dave Cooper        Each        £12.95

**COUNTRYWISE ONE**  Raymond Rush & Gavin Clowes        ISBN 1 897949 26 X        £ 6.95

**COUNTRYWISE TWO**  Raymond Rush & Gavin Clowes        ISBN 1 897949 65 0        £ 6.95
The meaning of country ways and words - featured on TV in "What's in a Word?"

**THE PEOVER EYE** John Lea        2003  Fishing and natural history memories
Limited edition 975 copies hardback with colour plates        ISBN 1 904546 01 3        £14.95

**WHITE PEAK MEMORIES:CLAUDE**  Claude Fearns        ISBN 1904546 04 8        £ 8.95

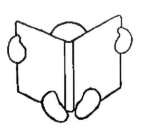